Her Restless Heart

A Woman's Longing for Love and Acceptance

A Faith and Fiction
B I B L E   S T U D Y

with

BARBARA CAMERON

Lori Jones, Contributor

Abingdon Press
Nashville

HER RESTLESS HEART:
A Woman's Longing for Love and Acceptance

Copyright © 2013 Abingdon Women

This book is printed on acid-free paper.

ISBN 978-1-4267-6170-6

Manufactured in the United States of America

13 14 15 16 17 18 19 20 21 22—10 9 8 7 6 5 4 3 2 1

Contents

Introduction

Do you have a restless heart? Are you discontent or unhappy with where you are or unsure about where you're headed? Do you feel stuck—reluctant to make necessary changes because you are afraid of what might come next? Maybe you can't put your finger on it; you just know you long for something more.

Whether or not you're in the midst of an obvious season of restlessness, the truth is that you do have a restless heart—we all do! We all know the longing within for something more. As women, our hearts are deep and complex—full of joy, love, sorrow, pain, and so many other emotions. Yet all of these emotions point to one simple and universal desire: to find real and lasting love and acceptance. We want to experience love, full and complete, and we want to know that we are accepted for who we are—that we are free to be who we were made to be. Though we tend to look to people and things to fulfill this longing, we can never know true love and acceptance—or complete freedom—until we are able to rest in God's unconditional, all-encompassing love and to trust His plan for our lives.

This study invites us on a journey in which we will explore the depths of our hearts and allow God to satisfy our restlessness, offering us His love, acceptance, and peace. Together we will walk through our doubts and fears and find healing for our hearts—as well as our relationships. We will discover what it means to live a life of freedom by living in God's love, and we will celebrate the God who is devoted to transforming us and blessing us beyond anything we ever dared to dream or imagine.

What makes this study unique is that it uses Christian fiction as a backdrop to explore biblical themes. Through the characters in *Her Restless Heart* and their stories, we will learn how resting in God's great love for us frees us to experience His joy and peace. The hope is that this refreshing approach of combining Bible study with narrative storytelling not only will enrich and enhance your study of God's Word, but also will help you to better understand and apply what you're learning in your own life as you relate to the characters and their experiences.

Everything needed to complete the study is provided in this workbook and your weekly group experience, in which you will watch a short video segment providing background information and insights into the story, themes, and

characters. Reading the novel is not required. However, if you would enjoy reading the book as you make your way through the study, you will find that this enhances your overall experience.

Whether reading the novel or only the excerpts and character sketches provided in this workbook, over the next six weeks you will come to know the characters in this story and the life challenges and healing journeys that each experiences. The story revolves around Mary Katherine, a young Amish woman who is caught between the traditions of her faith and the pull of a different life. As she struggles with her restless heart and seeks to find her place in the world, she finds herself faced with difficult choices in love and in life. Her journey illuminates the universal restlessness and longing of the human heart for satisfaction and fulfillment. As you journey with Mary Katherine, you will explore the themes of desire, woundedness, insecurity, grace, decision making, relationships, community, transformation, new beginnings, and the goodness of God—all through a biblical framework encompassing both the Old and New Testaments.

This workbook contains a book summary of *Her Restless Heart*, along with several character sketches of the main characters and a glossary of Amish terms used in the novel. This introductory material is titled "Before You Begin." You will want to read this material before beginning the study, especially if you do not plan to read the novel.

Each week of study begins with a Scripture for the week and an excerpt from the novel, setting the stage for the five readings that follow. Each day's reading may be completed in approximately 20-30 minutes. As you make your way through these readings, you will encounter additional excerpts from the novel offering insights related to the respective themes, commentary on selected Scriptures, and personal application.

The interactive format guides you through the material, providing questions for reflection and response throughout each reading. You will have the opportunity to share some of these responses when you gather with your small group. Writing your thoughts in the space provided will prepare you for the weekly group sessions as well as capture the insights you are gaining on your journey.

Each day's reading concludes with an "As You Go" suggestion for the day—a question to ponder, a Scripture to consider, or some action to take. Then, at the end of each week's readings, you will find a special "About the Amish" section, answering common questions about Amish customs, traditions, and practices.

I am excited to walk alongside you as we take this journey together. May God bless you with His love, mercy, and grace all along the way.

Barbara Cameron

Before You Begin

A Summary of *Her Restless Heart*

Mary Katherine is a young Amish woman who is struggling with the dream of a life different from the one she has always known.

Growing up in the Old Order Amish community of Paradise, Pennsylvania, Mary Katherine has lived a typical, simple Amish lifestyle on her family's farm. But her father's quick temper and harsh tongue, combined with her mother's meekness and submissive attitude, make Mary Katherine's growing-up years hard for her, and as soon as she is old enough, she seeks refuge in the home of her kind and wise grandmother, Leah.

It is in Leah's shop, Stitches in Time, that Mary Katherine finds her true passion and her heart's work in the craft of weaving. She excels in her art and it brings her happiness, but some in her strict Amish community have trouble appreciating the value of "decorative" arts, placing farming and other essential domestic pursuits above those they consider frivolous.

In her *rumschpringe*, Mary Katherine faces an important decision: whether to join the church and commit to her community for life or leave her community to live the life of an *Englischer* and become an outsider. Mary Katherine isn't sure what to do. She knows that she is loved and supported by many in her community, but her childhood has made her averse to the idea of becoming a docile Amish wife. And, deep down, she is struggling to trust God, feeling that He abandoned her in her family situation that was far from perfect.

As Mary Katherine struggles with her restless heart and seeks to find her place in the world, she finds herself faced with difficult choices in life—and in love. Though she isn't interested in dating anyone, when her longtime friend Jacob begins to show interest in pursuing her, she can't help but be intrigued by his kind, sensitive demeanor. Jacob is a farmer and loves what he does, but he also encourages Mary Katherine in her weaving. Though Jacob is a wonderful man and treats her with a winning attentiveness, her aversion to farming and to becoming a farm wife compels Mary Katherine to keep Jacob at arm's length, even as she feels her heart growing more and more fond of him. When Daniel, an old childhood

acquaintance, visits from Florida, Mary Katherine imagines what life might be like if she left Paradise behind. Daniel is a member of a more modern, less restrictive Beachy Amish Mennonite order in Florida. Once again, she is thrust into confusion over the state of her future—should she marry Jacob and finally settle into her community, or leave the only life she's ever known?

As Mary Katherine languishes in her indecision, her mother, Miriam, suffers an apparent heart attack, and Mary Katherine returns to her childhood home to help care for her mother. Being in her parents' home once again forces Mary Katherine to face the strained relationship she has with her parents, particularly with her father. Mary Katherine feels that she is a disappointment in his eyes, and she struggles to want to have a better relationship with him and to forgive him for the hurt he has caused her over the years. Mostly, she tries to avoid him, but in a moment of frustration and anger, Mary Katherine stands up to her father, and their confrontation causes him to realize just how domineering he has been with her and her mother over the years. Slowly Isaac's heart begins to turn, and Mary Katherine journeys toward reconciliation with him and with her mother.

Throughout the ordeal with her parents, Mary Katherine finds her relationship with Jacob steadily growing. Jacob continually surprises her with his kindness and gentleness, and she begins to realize that she is in love and desires a relationship with him.

Surrounded by unconditional love and encouragement from the women in her life—her grandmother, Leah, cousins Naomi and Anna, and her Englisch friend, Jamie—Mary Katherine's restlessness begins to settle, and she comes to feel God's love for her and to recognize His provision in her life. Mary Katherine decides that she wants to stay in the community and join the church. She excitedly heads to see Jacob to tell him the good news, but when she gets there, Mary Katherine finds Jacob reeling in jealousy because someone has told him Mary Katherine and Daniel were seen together the day before. He questions her intentions toward him, and Mary Katherine is furious that Jacob would think such a thing about her. Though he realizes his mistake and asks for forgiveness, her hurt leads her into fear that Jacob will hurt her as her father has. She instinctively pulls away from Jacob, but he continues to pursue her.

Finally Mary Katherine realizes that she does love Jacob and wants a life with him, and that she has to let go of her fear and indecision and trust God in order to move forward in her life. She finally is able to tell Jacob that she loves him, and she gratefully and happily accepts his love in return. Excited to start a new life, Mary Katherine and Jacob make plans for her to join the church and for them to marry.

Character Sketches

Mary Katherine

The heroine of the novel, Mary Katherine is searching for what she feels is her place in the world—not only the Amish or *Englisch* world, but also her own world. A gifted weaver, she hated working on the family farm with her autocratic father; now she revels in her relationships with her supportive grandmother, Leah; her two cousins, Naomi and Anna; and their Englisch friend, Jamie. Mary Katherine thrives at her grandmother's shop, Stitches in Time, but when her mother falls ill, she briefly returns to the farm to care for her mother, knowing that she will be facing her father's disapproval again. Watching the way her father has treated her mother as a subservient slave has made Mary Katherine wary of men, and so she keeps Jacob, a young man who's interested in her, at arm's length. Mary Katherine represents the inner child in all of us who wants to be loved for herself, not for what she can do for others. She struggles with committing herself to the church she has attended all her life and with dating Jacob, because she fears he'll try to control her like her father controlled her mother. But her biggest struggle is learning to know deep inside that God loves her and, because of this, that all will be well.

Leah (Mary Katherine's grandmother)

Wise and nurturing, Leah is able to help her granddaughters come to their own wisdom instead of trying to be the one who imparts it. (Her character was influenced by a coworker from my past, who got a call from her daughter when she was trying to make a difficult decision. Instead of this coworker telling her daughter what to do, she asked her what she thought she should do. Then she listened. When the daughter was finished, she said, "I think you made a good decision." That is how Leah approaches things.) When one of her granddaughters approaches her for advice, she listens, remarking on some things the granddaughter says. Then the young woman usually comes to self-wisdom/an epiphany about what's been troubling her.

Wisdom hasn't come easily to Leah. Widowed at a young age, she opened Stitches in Time to support herself and invited several of her grandchildren (Mary Katherine, Naomi, and Anna) to work with her and nurture their creative abilities. Leah has watched the troubled relationship Mary Katherine has with her father for years, but as much as she'd like to fix their problems, she knows they must come to a resolution themselves.

Naomi

Naomi is Mary Katherine's cousin who quilts (and the heroine of Book 2 in The Stitches in Time Series). Because the Amish have big families (the average

Amish family has seven children) she has many cousins, but she has always felt that she, Mary Katherine, and Anna are more like sisters. Naomi has come from a happier home than Mary Katherine, but she places too much importance on pleasing the young man who is courting her. It isn't long before she realizes that she has given up some of her self-esteem to gain his love and approval (Book 2).

Anna

A young widow (and the heroine of Book 3 in The Stitches in Time Series), Anna pretends that she has dealt with the loss of her beloved husband. Often she acts the opposite of how she feels and teases her cousins Mary Katherine and Naomi. But she is struggling with feelings of loss and loneliness and spends too much time knitting items for the Stitches in Time shop. She reflects on the irony of her talent in knitting baby caps because she did not have children with her husband, and she tries not to think about whether she will ever have a second chance at love.

Jacob

The hero of the story, Jacob owns a farm that has been passed down through many generations. Unlike Mary Katherine, he knows where he belongs and what he wants—a future with her. But Jacob has to learn some new ways when he makes a thoughtless comment to one of his sisters about cooking ("How hard can it be?"), and he learns new respect for what the women of his family do. Even though he is a man who is down to earth and practical, one who works to grow crops, he understands Mary Katherine and her talent better than anyone else except Leah. When he witnesses for himself how Mary Katherine is treated by her father and sees the relationship her parents have, he knows he must show her that he loves her and convince her that they will have a strong and happy marriage.

Daniel

Daniel is a secondary love interest who is a symbol of escape for Mary Katherine: if she chooses to become interested in him, she can escape to a place she sees as having more freedom for her (Florida). Daniel, owner of a landscape company, is a member of the Beachy Amish Mennonite group in Pinecraft, Florida, near Sarasota. His is a more relaxed church group than her Old Order Amish church family, and that is attractive to Mary Katherine, who has chafed at the restrictions in Paradise. Daniel, Mary Katherine, and Jacob grew up together, and when Daniel shows interest in Mary Katherine, Jacob worries that he'll lose her to Daniel and his freer lifestyle in Florida. (Daniel also represents Mary Katherine's difficulty in making decisions for her life.)

Isaac (Mary Katherine's father)

Isaac is a very traditional Amish man who works hard to farm his land and stay true to strict, Old Order Amish tenets. He has no sons, so he has been harder and harsher with his daughter, Mary Katherine, when he needed help with farm work. Although he has never struck Mary Katherine, he doesn't realize that his words wound her and Miriam, his devoted wife. Isaac feels there is just one way—his—and so he drives away his only daughter and saddens his wife, Miriam. Stuck in the beliefs and authoritarian role he believes is correct, he changes when he realizes that behaving this way may mean that he will lose his daughter, Mary Katherine, and his wife completely.

Miriam (Mary Katherine's mother)

Miriam is meek and submissive, and she has quietly accepted less-than-kind and less-than-loving behavior from her husband, Isaac, for years. She has been miserable watching him drive away their only daughter, but she feels she cannot speak up. She longs to have Mary Katherine near but is happy that she is thriving and creating beautiful work at Stitches in Time. Even when she suffers a heart attack, she doesn't speak up and say that things need to be different—that her unhappiness is affecting her health. She learns from Mary Katherine's example that she must change what she accepts if she wants things to be different.

Jamie

Jamie is a college student and Englisch friend of Mary Katherine. Jamie has experienced many of the same issues with her parents as Mary Katherine, so they have more in common than might be obvious at first. But Jamie has been able to speak up, to attend college, and to learn about people and relationships there. She and Mary Katherine talk often about their love for creating. From the time that Jamie wanders into Stitches in Time, looking for fabrics and supplies for her classes (she wants to be a fabric artist) and talking with Mary Katherine, they become sisters of the heart. Eventually Jamie is hired as a part-time worker at Stitches in Time.

Glossary

Ach—oh (exclamation)
Allrecht—all right

Daed—dad
Danki—thank you
Dat—father
Der Hochmut kummt vor dem Fall—Pride goeth before the fall

Englischer—non-Amish people

Fraa—wife

Grossmudder—grandmother
Guder mariye*—Good morning
Gut—good
Gut-n-owed—Good evening

Haus*—house
Hochmut—pride

Kapp—prayer covering or cap worn by girls and women
Kind, kinner—child, children
Kumm—come

Liebschen—dearest or dear one

Mamm—mother

Nee—no

Ordnung—The rules of the Amish, both written and unwritten. Certain behavior has been expected within the Amish community for many, many years. These rules vary from community to community, but the most common direct the Amish not to have electricity in the home, not to own or drive an automobile, and to dress a certain way.

Rotrieb—red beet

Rumschpringe—Time period when teenagers are allowed to experience the Englisch world while deciding if they should join the church. The length of time ranges in different communities but usually starts around age sixteen and ends in the mid-twenties.

Schul—school
Schur—sure

Wunderbaar*—wonderful

Ya—yes

*Used in the novel but not in the excerpts in this book.

Week 1
The Hungry Heart

Scripture for the Week

Give thanks to the LORD, for he is good;
his love endures forever. . . .
Let them give thanks to the LORD for his unfailing love
and his wonderful deeds for mankind,
for he satisfies the thirsty
and fills the hungry with good things.

Psalm 107:1, 8-9

Setting the Stage

The heart of a woman is a wild and wonderful thing. It is prone to burst with joy, to sicken with heartbreak, to grow with compassion. Our hearts long for many things, but above all they long for love and acceptance. They long to trust and to be trusted, to be filled to capacity with peace and contentment. And though we search for fulfillment in the people and places around us, our hearts long for the complete love that only God can give.

This week we will uncover the natural longings of our hearts and explore how our misplaced desires can often leave us restless and confused. We will discover how God's gift of perfect love offers us peace and hope.

Excerpt from Chapter 1

A year ago, Mary Katherine wouldn't have imagined she'd be here. Back then, she'd been helping her parents on the family farm and hating every minute of it.

Now, she stood at the front window of Stitches in Time, her grandmother's shop, watching the Englischers *moving about on the sidewalks outside the shop in Paradise. Even on vacation, they rushed about with purpose. She imagined them*

checking off the places they'd visited: Drive by an Amish farmhouse. Check. Buy a quilt and maybe some knitting supplies to try making a sweater when I get back home. Check.

She liked the last item. The shop had been busy all morning, but now, as people started getting hungry, they were patronizing the restaurants that advertised authentic Amish food and ticking off another item on their vacation checklist. Shoofly pie. Amish pretzels. Chow-chow. Check.

"Don't you worry, they'll be back," Leah, her grandmother, called out.

Smiling, Mary Katherine turned. "I know."

She wandered back to the center of the shop, set up like the comfortable parlor of an Amish farmhouse. Chairs were arranged in a circle around a quilting frame. Bolts of fabric of every color and print imaginable were stacked on shelves on several walls, spools of matching threads on another.

And yarn. There were skeins and skeins of the stuff. Mary Katherine loved running her hands over the fluffy fibers, feeling the textures of cotton and wool and silk. Some of the new yarns made from things like soybeans and corn just didn't feel the same when you knitted them or wove them into patterns—but some people made a fuss over them because they were made of something natural, plant-based, or more sustainable.

Mary Katherine thought it was a little strange to be using vegetables you ate to make clothes but once she got her hands on the yarns, she was impressed. Tourists were, too. They used terms like "green" and "ecological" and didn't mind spending a lot of money to buy them. And was it so much different to use vegetables when people had been taking oily, smelly wool from sheep and turning it into garments for people—silk from silkworms—that sort of thing?

"You have that look on your face again," her grandmother said.

"What look?"

"That serious, thoughtful look of yours. Tell me what you're thinking of."

"Working on my loom this afternoon."

"I figured you had itchy fingers." Her grandmother smiled.

She sighed. "I'm so glad you rescued me from working at the farm. And Dat *not understanding about my weaving."*

Leah nodded. "Some people need time to adjust."

Taking one of the chairs that was arranged in a circle around the quilt her grandmother and Naomi worked on, Mary Katherine propped her chin in her hand, her elbow on the arm of the chair. "It'd be a lot easier if I knitted or quilted."

Leah looked at her, obviously suppressing a smile. "You have never liked 'easy,' Mary Katherine."

Laughing, she nodded. "You're right."

Looking at Naomi and Anna, her cousins aged twenty and twenty-three, was like looking into a mirror, thought Mary Katherine. The three of them could have

been sisters, not cousins. They had a similar appearance—oval faces, their hair center-parted and tucked back under snowy white kapps, and slim figures. Naomi and Anna had even chosen dresses of a similar color, one that reminded Mary Katherine of morning glories. In her rush out the door, Mary Katherine had grabbed the first available dress and now felt drab and dowdy in the brown dress she'd chosen.

Yes, they looked much alike, the three of them.

Until Mary Katherine stood. She'd continued growing after it seemed that everyone else had stopped. Now, at 5'8", she felt like a skinny beanpole next to her cousins. She felt awkward next to the young men she'd gone to school with. Although she knew it was wrong, there had been times when she'd secretly wished that God had made her petite and pretty like her cousins. And why had he chosen to give her red hair and freckles? Didn't she have enough she didn't like about her looks without that?

Like their looks, their personalities seemed similar on the surface. The three of them appeared calm and serene—especially Naomi. Anna tried to be, but it didn't last long. She was too mischievous.

And herself? Serenity seemed hard these days. In the past several years, Mary Katherine had been a little moody but lately it seemed her moods were going up and down like a road through rolling hills.

"Feeling restless?" Naomi asked, looking at her with concern. Nimbly, she tied a knot, snipped the thread with a scissors, then slid her needle into a pincushion.

Anna looked up from her knitting needles. "Mary Katherine was born restless."

"I think I'll take a short walk."

"No," Leah said quickly, holding up a hand. "Let's eat first, then you can take a walk. Otherwise you'll come back and customers will be here for the afternoon rush and you'll start helping and go hungry."

Mary Katherine was already mentally out the door, but she nodded her agreement. "You're right, of course."

Leah was a tall, spare woman who didn't appear old enough to be anyone's grandmother. Her face was smooth and unlined, and there wasn't a trace of gray in her hair, which she wore like her granddaughters.

"I made your favorite," Leah told Mary Katherine.

"Fried chicken? You made fried chicken? When did you have time to do that?"

Nodding, Leah tucked away her sewing supplies, and stood. "Before we came to work this morning. It didn't take long." She turned to Naomi. "And I made your favorite."

Naomi had been picking up stray strands of yarn from the wood floor. She looked up, her eyes bright. "Macaroni and cheese?"

"Oatmeal and raisin cookies?" Anna wanted to know. When her grandmother

"Feeling restless?" Naomi asked, looking at her with concern.... Anna looked up from her knitting needles. "Mary Katherine was born restless."

17

nodded, Anna set down her knitting needles and stood. "Just how early did you get up? Are you having trouble sleeping?"

"No earlier than usual," Leah replied cheerfully. "I made the macaroni and cheese and the cookies last night. But I don't need as much sleep as some other people I know."

"Can you blame me for sleeping in a little later?" Mary Katherine asked. "After all of those years of helping with farm chores? Besides, I was working on a design last night."

"Tell us all about it while we eat," Naomi said, glancing at the clock. "We won't have long before customers start coming in again." . . .

The minute they finished eating, Mary Katherine jumped up and hurried over to wash her dishes. "I'll be right back," she promised, tying her bonnet on the run as she left the store.

Winter's chill was in the air. She shivered a little but didn't want to go back for her shawl. She shrugged. Once she got moving, she'd be warm enough.

She felt the curious stares as if she were touched.

But that was okay. Mary Katherine was doing a lot of staring of her own. She had a great deal of curiosity about the Englisch and didn't mind admitting it.

She just hoped that her grandmother didn't know how much she'd thought about becoming one of them, of not being baptized into the Amish church.

As one of the tourists walked past, a pretty woman about her own age, Mary Katherine wondered what it felt like being covered in so little clothing. She suspected she'd feel half-naked in that dress she'd heard called a sundress. Although some of the tourists looked surprised when she and her cousins wore bright colors, the fact was that the Ordnung certainly didn't mandate black dresses.

Color had always been part of Mary Katherine's world. She'd loved all the shades of blue because they reminded her of the big blue bowl of the sky. Her father had complained that she didn't get her chores done in a timely manner because she was always walking around . . . noticing. She noticed everything around her, absorbed the colors and textures, and spent hours using them in her designs that didn't look like the quilts and crafts other Amish women created.

She paused at the display window of Stitches in Time. A wedding ring quilt that Naomi had sewn was draped over a quilt rack. Anna had knitted several darling little cupcake hats for babies to protect their heads and ears from the cold. And there was her own woven throw made of many different fibers and textures and colors of burnt orange, gold, brown, and green. All echoed the theme of the colder seasons, of the weddings that would come after summer harvests.

And all were silent testament to Leah's belief in the creativity of her granddaughters, thought Mary Katherine with a smile. The shop featured the traditional crafts tourists might expect but also the new directions the cousins came up with.

It was the best of both worlds Mary Katherine said to herself as she ventured out into the throng of tourists lining the sidewalks.

Jacob saw Mary Katherine exit her grandmother's shop. His timing was perfect because he'd heard from a secret source what time they took a break to eat at the shop during the day.

He watched her stop to gaze at the display window and she smiled—the smile that had attracted him to her. Oh, she was pretty with those big blue eyes and soft skin with a blush of rose over her cheekbones. But her smile.

She hadn't always smiled like that. He started noticing it just a few months ago, after the shop had opened. It was as if she'd come to life. He'd passed by the shop one day a couple of weeks ago and stopped to glance inside, and he'd seen her working at her loom, a look of absorption on her face, a quiet smile on her lips.

Something had moved in his chest then, a feeling he hadn't had before. He'd resolved to figure this out.

He hadn't been in a rush to marry. It had been enough to take over the family farm, to make sure he didn't undo all the hard work that his daed *had done to make it thrive. He didn't feel pride that he'd continued its success. After all, Plain people felt* hochmut *was wrong. In school, they had often practiced writing the proverb, "Der Hochmut kummt vor dem fall." Pride goeth before the fall.*

But the farm, its continuity, its legacy for the family he wanted one day . . . that was important to him. To have that family, he knew he'd have to find a fraa. *It was important to find the right one. After all, Plain people married for life. So he'd looked around but he had taken his time. He likened the process to a crop—you prepared the ground, planted the right seed, nurtured it, asked God's blessing, and then harvested at the right moment.*

Such things took time.

Sometimes they even took perseverance. She had turned him down when he'd approached her and asked her out.

He decided not to let that discourage him.

She turned from the window and began walking down the sidewalk toward him. Look at her, he thought, walking with that bounce to her step. Look at the way she glanced around, taking in everything with such animation, such curiosity.

He waited for some sign of recognition, but she hadn't seen him yet. When they'd attended school, their teacher had often gently chided her for staring out the classroom window or doodling designs on a scrap of paper for the weaving she loved.

Mary Katherine moved through the sea of Englisch *tourists on the sidewalk that parted for her when she walked as the waters had for Moses. He watched how they glanced at her the way she did them.*

It was a mutual curiosity at its best.

He walked toward her and when she stopped and blinked, he grinned.

"Jacob! What are you doing here?"

"You make it sound like I never come to town."

"I don't remember ever seeing you do it."

"I needed some supplies, and things are slower now with the harvest in. Have you eaten?" He'd found out from Anna when they took their noontime break, but he figured it was a good conversational device.

"Yes. We ate a little early at the shop."

He thought about that. Maybe he should have planned better. "I see. Well, how about having supper with me tonight?"

"Did you come all the way into town to ask me out?"

Jacob drew himself up. "Yes."

"But I've told you before—"

"That you're not interested in going out."

"Yes."

"But I haven't heard of you going out with anyone else."

She stared at him, oblivious of the people who streamed around them on the sidewalk. "Who did you ask?"

Her direct stare was unnerving. His collar felt tight, but he knew if he pulled it away from his neck he'd just appear guilty. "I'd have heard."

"I'm not interested in dating, Jacob."

When she started past him, he put out his hand to stop her. She looked down at his hand on her arm and then met his gaze. "Is it you're not interested in dating or you're not interested in dating me?"

Her lips quirked. "I'm not interested in dating. It's not you."

"I see."

She began walking again.

"Do you mind if I walk with you?"

"Schur." She glanced at him. "Can you keep up?"

He found himself grinning. She was different from other young women he knew, more spirited and independent.

"Where are we going?"

She shrugged. "Nowhere in particular. I just needed to get out and get some fresh air."

Stopping at a shop window, she studied its display of tourist souvenirs. "Did you ever think about not staying here? In Paradise?"

"Not stay here? Where would you go?"

She turned to look at him and shrugged. "I don't know. It's a big world out there."

Jacob felt a chill race up his spine. "You can't mean it," he said slowly. "You belong here."

"Do I?" she asked. Pensive, she stared at the people passing. "Sometimes I'm not sure where I belong."

Day 1: The Desire for More

Read God's Word

The Lord God took the man and put him in the Garden of Eden to work it and take care of it. And the Lord God commanded the man, "You are free to eat from any tree in the garden; but you must not eat from the tree of the knowledge of good and evil, for when you eat from it you will certainly die." The Lord God said, "It is not good for the man to be alone. I will make a helper suitable for him." . . .

Then the Lord God made a woman from the rib he had taken out of the man, and he brought her to the man.

Now the serpent was more crafty than any of the wild animals the Lord God had made. He said to the woman, "Did God really say, 'You must not eat from any tree in the garden'?"

The woman said to the serpent, "We may eat fruit from the trees in the garden, but God did say, 'You must not eat fruit from the tree that is in the middle of the garden, and you must not touch it, or you will die.'"

"You will not certainly die," the serpent said to the woman. "For God knows that when you eat from it your eyes will be opened, and you will be like God, knowing good and evil."

When the woman saw that the fruit of the tree was good for food and pleasing to the eye, and also desirable for gaining wisdom, she took some

and ate it. She also gave some to her husband, who was with her, and he ate it. Then the eyes of both of them were opened.

Genesis 2:15-18, 22; 3:1-7a

Reflect and Respond

From the very beginning of time, we humans have struggled with the desire for *more*. More knowledge, more beauty, more pleasure, more power, more fulfillment.

Adam and Eve walked with God Himself in the most perfect environment possible. It was a breathtakingly beautiful place. God provided for their every need. They had companionship and important work. What more could they want?

But somewhere in the recesses of Eve's mind there was a question: *What if there is more?* A few words from a crafty serpent opened the floodgates of temptation, and an act of disobedience forever altered humankind's relationship with God.

> Our hearts and minds are filled with longings that we can rarely name, but that we feel down deep in the core of our being.

What do you imagine the Garden of Eden looked like? How do you imagine its beauty affected the senses—what did it smell like, how did its fruit taste, what sounds would you have heard, what textures would you have felt, what beauty might your eyes have seen?

Read Genesis 3:7-13. How do these verses describe how Adam and Eve reacted after they ate the fruit of the tree? What do you imagine their immediate reaction was—what might their thoughts have been? How do you think they viewed the Garden after that moment?

Adam and Eve lived in a literal paradise, their every need met and their every want answered. But they were restless, and when faced with a life-changing decision, they succumbed to that restlessness and longing for more.

We aren't so different from Adam and Eve, are we? Our hearts and minds are filled with longings that we can rarely name, but that we feel down deep in the core of our being. We're unsatisfied with the world around us. We're frustrated with our relationships, which regularly fail to meet our expectations. We struggle to enjoy the work of our hands. We feel trapped by all the freedoms we're supposed to enjoy.

What do we really want? Why are we so unsatisfied?

Though she enjoys the fruitful work of her hands and rich relationships with the women in her life, Mary Katherine is restless in Paradise, Pennsylvania. She isn't sure that she fits in with the community around her and is unsure she can live up to their expectations, but at the same time she desperately wants to find her place in the world.

Have you ever felt like Mary Katherine does—restless and unsure where you fit into the world around you? What was the situation, and how did you react?

What factors do you think contributed to your restlessness in that situation? What was going on in your heart at the time?

Read Genesis 3:16-19. As a result of Adam and Eve's disobedience, what happened to their companionship with God? What are the lasting effects of their restlessness on humankind?

Though Adam and Eve's sin created a chasm in the relationship between them and their Creator, God did not abandon them in their time of confusion and bad choices. After eating the fruit of the Tree of the Knowledge of Good and Evil and breaking God's commandment, the pair immediately realized they were naked, exposed. They were afraid and humiliated. And though their actions saddened their Lord and broke their relationship with Him, even in that moment He cared for them. Genesis 3:21 says, "The LORD God made garments of skin for Adam and his wife and clothed them."

God our Father, our Protector, who is omniscient (all-knowing) and omni-present (all-present), knows that our hearts long for more than what we have. He knows that although we search and worry and fret, our hearts will never be satisfied until they rest in the assurance of His perfect love. And in the midst of our longing, He cares for us.

Talk to God

Heavenly Father, from the beginning of time You have cared for us and pursued us with Your patient love. You are not surprised by my selfish longings and fruitless wanderings, but You patiently and continually draw my heart to You. Thank You for Your grace and love, Father. Help me to rest in that today. Amen.

As You Go

As you go about your day today, pay attention to the desires and longings you experience throughout the day. What do you daydream about? What makes you angry? What makes you laugh? What makes you cry?

Day 2: Prone to Restlessness

Read God's Word

"Be still, and know that I am God; I will be exalted among the nations, I will be exalted in the earth."

Psalm 46:10

Reflect and Respond

One Sunday in church I noticed a small child who was sitting with his family. Positioned between the mother and father, I could see the back of his small head peeking up from in front of the pew and his legs dangling below. As the pastor began his sermon, the parents glanced down with knowing looks, seeming to remind him of the instructions they'd coached him in before the service started. *Be still. Be quiet.*

And he was still and quiet—for a while. After a few minutes I saw his little foot start to swing back and forth, gently at first, and then faster and harder. Before long I could see both legs swinging in earnest. Soon his whole body was rocking back and forth with the momentum; his parents exchanged worried glances, no doubt wondering which one of them would need to take him outside so that he didn't disturb anyone.

He had tried to be still—really, he had. But he just couldn't take it anymore. The wiggle worms infiltrated his little body and took over.

Often we hear the words of the Lord: "Be still, and know that I am God." And we say, "Yes, Lord, you are in control and I am not; I can rest now." But before we know it, there is a growing restlessness in our spirits, telling us that maybe there is more, maybe we need to do more, be more, find more—and before long we are wiggling all over with fear and doubt and worry.

Are you currently experiencing any restlessness in your life? If so, in what areas?

How are you reacting to that restlessness in your emotions, thoughts, and actions?

Some days we may experience a strong, almost physical restlessness that causes us to explode in anger or frustration. But most often we live with a quiet restlessness. We have a vague sense that something's wrong, but we aren't sure what it is exactly or how to fix it. The ambiguity and uncertainty causes us to question everything—our faith, our marriages, our work, our environments—in a desperate search to find the broken piece and repair it or change it altogether.

Naomi jokes that Mary Katherine was "born restless." Do you think that certain personalities are prone to restlessness? Why or why not?

Would you consider yourself a restless personality? If so, in what ways?

Often we live with a quiet restlessness. We have a vague sense that something's wrong, but we aren't sure what it is exactly or how to fix it.

What are some reasons we as women are often restless? What emotional and cultural factors do you think contribute to this restlessness?

In many ways our culture is designed to keep us restless and unsatisfied. Constant advertisements sell us on the idea that something else is better than what we have. Our economy is fueled by competition and comparison. Being complacent—content—is frowned upon. The fear that being content will make us unproductive keeps us striving and working harder and harder. The idea of rest and stillness seems indulgent and lazy.

What emotions do the words *peace*, *rest*, and *stillness* evoke in you?

Read the following verses. What does the Bible say about rest in each verse?

Genesis 2:2

Mark 4:39

Matthew 11:28-29

Do you pursue peace, rest, and stillness in your own life? If so, how? If not, what takes precedence in your life, and how are those priorities affecting your life?

When Martin Luther was discouraged, he would say, "Come, let us sing the forty-sixth psalm."[1] Psalm 46 teaches us to take comfort in God when everything around us seems dim and threatening. When our emotions are on a rollercoaster and we can't see how a situation will work itself out, we are encouraged to trust in God's power and provision over our lives. This psalm beckons us to "Come and see what the LORD has done" (v. 8) and reminds us that we are watched over and protected.

Read Psalm 46 in its entirety.

In what ways is this psalm comforting and encouraging?

What do you think God means when He tells the psalmist, "Be still, and know that I am God"?

Talk to God

God, You are ruler of all. Thank You for the reminders that You have taken care of Your children throughout time, and You will take care of me. Help me to trust and rest in Your care and wisdom, and teach me how to let go of the things I hold so tightly to that I don't allow You to do Your perfect work. Help me to value rest and stillness, seeing them as a mark of someone who knows how to trust in Your love and protection. Amen.

As You Go

How might the command "Be still and know that I am God" affect an area of your life today? In what way will you choose to obey God's command to rest in the knowledge that He is in control?

Day 3: Finding Satisfaction

Read God's Word

The words of the Teacher, son of David, king in Jerusalem:

"Meaningless! Meaningless!" says the Teacher. "Utterly meaningless! Everything is meaningless."

What do people gain from all their labors at which they toil under the sun?

Generations come and generations go, but the earth remains forever.

The sun rises and the sun sets, and hurries back to where it rises.

The wind blows to the south and turns to the north; round and round it goes, ever returning on its course.

All streams flow into the sea, yet the sea is never full. To the place the streams come from, there they return again.

All things are wearisome, more than one can say. The eye never has enough of seeing, nor the ear its fill of hearing.

What has been will be again, what has been done will be done again; there is nothing new under the sun.

Is there anything of which one can say, "Look! This is something new"? It was here already, long ago; it was here before our time.

Ecclesiastes 1:1-10

It is sad not to get what you hoped for. But wishes that come true are like eating fruit from the tree of life.

Proverbs 13:12 NCV

> Though it seems as if our modern-day culture conspires to keep us restless and wanting more, our present dilemmas are nothing new to the condition of the human heart.

Reflect and Respond

Though it seems as if our modern-day culture conspires to keep us restless and wanting more, our present dilemmas are nothing new to the condition of the human heart. Consider the Old Testament book of Ecclesiastes. The author, King Solomon, was a king of great renown. The son of Israel's beloved King David, Solomon had restored the people's faith by building an amazing temple to be a place of worship and a home for the Ark of the Covenant (also known as God's presence). He was an extremely successful king by anyone's standards, and the world was seemingly at his fingertips. Solomon had everything that a man could acquire. And yet he was restless.

Ecclesiastes reads like a diary of sorts, chronicling Solomon's pursuit of fulfillment and meaning and joy. *Wisdom—check! Success—check! Wealth—check!* Solomon had all those things in spades, and yet he found that nothing he could acquire or attain could give him the deep and satisfying joy that he found when he finally realized he could rest in God's love, provision, and authority. Pursuing anything else, he said, is like "chasing the wind" (Ecclesiastes 1:17).

Why do we need the message of Ecclesiastes?

Read all of Ecclesiastes 1. How do you identify with Solomon's frustration in finding meaning in his life? Have you faced similar struggles of your own?

Centuries after Solomon lived, a young man named Augustine found himself struggling with the same frustrations and fruitless searches Solomon experienced. After living a life devoted first to seeking pleasure and then to seeking wisdom through various philosophical pursuits, Augustine finally discovered that a life of devotion to God and reveling in his status as God's child was the only thing that could truly satisfy. In his book *Confessions*, he wrote, "Thou hast formed us for Thyself, and our hearts are restless till they find rest in Thee."[2]

In what areas of your life do you seek fulfillment? Circle those that apply and write in any other areas.

Work

Family

Health

Friendships

Church

Other areas:

How have you been fulfilled and disappointed in these important areas of your life?

Write the first thing that comes to your mind when you read the following question: What do you most desire in your life?

What does your answer to the previous question reveal about where you are putting your hope?

Choosing to trust and live in God's love is the ultimate source of life and fulfillment for our hearts.

When Mary Katherine discovers her gift for weaving, she finds fulfillment in her work and receives much encouragement about its quality and beauty from customers, her grandmother, and her cousins. Although she is able to find joy and some peace in that area of her life, it does not fulfill a deeper desire—to experience unconditional love and acceptance from her family and her community. This desire, of course, is only a shadow of her heart's true and greatest desire, which is to know and experience the unconditional love and acceptance of God. Like Solomon, she discovers that the work of her hands cannot fulfill the deep desires of her heart.

Proverbs 13:12 says, "It is sad not to get what you hoped for. But wishes that come true are like eating fruit from the tree of life" (NCV). Both King Solomon and Saint Augustine discovered through their experience and disappointment that choosing to trust and live in God's love is the ultimate source of life and fulfillment for our hearts. Anything else will be less than what we've hoped for.

God's gift of complete love and acceptance required no small sacrifice. John 3:16 says, "For God so loved the world that he gave his one and only Son, that whoever believes in him shall not perish but have eternal life." God sent His Son, Jesus, to Earth to become the sacrifice for our sins and pave the way for us to have an intimate relationship with Him. Trusting in that sacrifice and reveling in our state as God's beloved children is the only way our hearts will find fulfillment during our short time here on Earth. He is the only One who can fulfill the complete desires of our hearts.

God's salvation and grace is a gift to us—there is nothing we can do to earn the gift, and there is nothing we can add to or take away from it. All we need to do is open our hands to the gift of His love and accept it—gratefully and eagerly. It is a perfect gift, and in His love we will find rest for our hungry hearts.

Romans 3:23 says that "all have sinned and fall short of the glory of God." In other words, we don't deserve His grace, but Jesus gives it anyway. Have you accepted God's gift of grace in your life?

Do you believe that God is enough to fulfill you? Why or why not?

Sometimes we acknowledge that we believe God is enough, but the way we tend to live our lives reveals what we functionally believe— that other things can fill the void. What does the way you live your life reveal about what you believe to be true?

Talk to God

Dear God, thank You for the amazing, incomparable gift of Your love and mercy. That is all I can say—thank You. I wholeheartedly accept Your gift and celebrate what You've done for me. May my life be a reflection of the great gift I've been given, and may I be eager to share Your light and love with others. Amen.

As You Go

Spend some time prayerfully considering the answer you wrote in response to the question about what you most desire in life. Ask God to reveal to you what is behind the answer you gave, and how you can find satisfaction for that desire in Him.

Day 4: God Provides and Satisfies

Read God's Word

Give thanks to the LORD, for he is good;
his love endures forever. . . .
Let them give thanks to the LORD for his unfailing love
and his wonderful deeds for mankind,
for he satisfies the thirsty
and fills the hungry with good things.

Psalm 107:1, 8-9

Reflect and Respond

Most of us do not encounter the physical experience of being hungry often. Sure, we are sometimes too busy to stop what we're doing to slow down and eat an actual meal. Our stomachs growl a bit and protest, so we grab a few handfuls of whatever snack we can find and push through the mild hunger until we can enjoy a good meal later.

Though it is likely few of us have ever experienced the debilitating hunger that many people in our world face on a daily basis, many of us suffer from having hungry hearts—hearts that are weakened by complacency and exhausted by doubt and disappointment. And yet we sit at a table where a feast has been placed before us, where God has provided us with more love, assurance, grace, mercy, and joy than we could ever take in. He has given us His salvation, which quenches our thirst for acceptance. He has offered us a place at His table, which fulfills our hunger for love.

But too often we sit at the table and remain hungry. We sit and look at the offerings before us, praising their beauty and imagining how amazing it would be to enjoy them, but we hold back from devouring all the goodness before us. Instead of indulging ourselves, we wonder if the feast is really for us. We wonder how we will compensate for what we take. We are afraid of how the feast might change us. And so we sit and appreciate what we see but leave the table unchanged.

Second Peter 1:3 says, "[God's] divine power has given us everything we need for life and godliness." God has given us His love and His

grace—everything that we need to fulfill the deepest longings of our hearts. Why, then, do you think we still tend to have restless hearts?

Are there any of God's gifts—any provisions from His table—that you have a hard time partaking of? Why do you think that is?

When we listen to our doubts and fears, sometimes it can be hard to hear God's still, steady, gentle voice in our lives. As Mary Katherine's decision to join the church weighs heavy on her, she confesses that she's not sure what God is leading her to do and asks her wise and loving grandmother, Leah, for advice about seeking God's will for her life.

Excerpt from Chapter 4

Uh-oh, here it comes, Mary Katherine thought. She's got that look on her face.

"Have you thought any more about getting baptized?" [Leah] asked after a long moment.

It was so hard to disappoint her grandmother. But she just wasn't ready to do it yet. She wasn't even sure she would ever be ready.

"You know this isn't about having a wild rumschpringe, *trying out alcohol, or being wild, all that—"*

"Of course not," Leah interrupted her quickly.

"I'm sorry," she began. "I'm just not ready—"

"No, I don't want you to be sorry," Leah rushed to say. "I don't mean to pressure you."

"It's a big decision," she said, struggling to find the words, feeling her way. "If I joined the church, you know what would happen if I changed my mind and left. I'd be shunned—"

Leah waved her hands. "No, don't even use that word. I don't want to hear it. You wouldn't leave once you'd joined!"

Mary Katherine rubbed her temple. "I just feel like I don't know where I belong yet."

Leah turned pale. "You're not seriously thinking of becoming Englisch." *She made it a statement, not a question. "I know you chafed at the rules sometimes growing up, that your* dat *was stricter with you than I thought he should be. But you're not really drawn to the* Englisch *life, are you?"*

When we listen to our doubts and fears, sometimes it can be hard to hear God's still, steady, gentle voice in our lives.

She hesitated. "There are freedoms . . ." Emotions welled up inside her. "You know me better than anyone. Yes, I chafed at the rules growing up, and yes, oh yes, my father was stricter than you thought he should be. He was—he was—" she stopped, struggled for composure. "He was so, so much stricter than you'll ever know."

Than she would ever tell her grandmother, she thought.

"Mary Katherine—"

She shook her head. "No, I don't want to talk about it. It's done now. It's over. But I need some time."

"It's been a year since you left your parents and came to live with me and work here."

"Not enough. Not nearly enough." She sighed.

"Have you asked God for direction?" Leah asked gently.

"God doesn't listen to me." She heard the bitter disappointment in her voice.

"Sometimes He talks to us and we hear Him instantly, loud and clear," her grandmother said. "Sometimes He's soft and He whispers, and we almost miss Him. And sometimes He speaks through other people."

She leaned back in her seat. "I remember the first time that God spoke loudly to me. Scared me half to death."

"What happened?"

"I was driving the buggy home one evening. The kinner were asleep in the back. Suddenly this voice said, 'Pull over! A drunk driver's coming!' Well, I thought one of the kinner was playing a joke, being a ventriloquist. You know, throwing his voice, making it sound deeper. I glanced into the backseat and everyone was asleep. Then I glanced up and there were headlights from a car coming straight into my side of the road. I pulled the buggy over onto the grassy shoulder just in time."

Mary Katherine stared at her, wide-eyed. "You never told me that before."

"Well, you never know if someone will believe you about that sort of thing if they haven't experienced it. Besides, if God never speaks that loudly to them, they might think there's something wrong with their faith."

Maybe there was something wrong with her faith, Mary Katherine thought. She couldn't remember a time when she felt God talked to her.

Has there ever been a time in your life when you clearly heard God's voice speaking to you? Was it audible or something you just sensed in your spirit? What did He say?

In the life of a believer, there will be times when we hear and feel clear direction from God and other times when it seems that God is silent. In those times of silence, we can't help but wonder, *Is God listening to me?*

Read the following verses and note what each has to say about God's attention toward His children.

Psalm 34:17

1 John 5:14

Hebrews 13:5

Scripture repeatedly tells us that God is listening and that He hears the cries of His children.

Like Mary Katherine, we may sometimes wonder if God is silent because we are doing something wrong or because we don't have enough faith to warrant His attention. But Scripture repeatedly tells us that God is listening and that He hears the cries of His children. He will not leave us stranded and alone. He is committed to our good, and He desires for us to follow Him.

James 1:17 says, "There is nothing deceitful in God, nothing two-faced, nothing fickle" (*THE MESSAGE*). Though our doubts can shout loudly and our fear and weakness dim our hearing, what we feel does not change who God is.

Do you ever have doubts that God is who the Bible says He is? What do you tend to do when you doubt?

Hebrews 13:8 says, "Jesus Christ is the same yesterday and today and forever." How does this verse speak to your doubts and fears? What do you hear God telling you through this verse?

God *is* the same yesterday and today and forever. So when we are discouraged and seeking direction, we should run to our Father and to His table. We can be confident that He is Who He says He is, and that His gifts are for the taking. We can confidently celebrate His love for us and rest in the knowledge that we are His beloved children and that He delights in us.

Talk to God

Father, today I run to Your table, eager to fill my hungry heart with You. I praise You for Your good and gracious gifts. When I am restless and afraid, help me to turn my eyes toward You. Fill me with Your love and peace, and sustain me with the knowledge that I am Your beloved child. Amen.

As You Go

Today when you eat your meals, remind yourself that God is your provider, and that He provides for your physical needs as well as the deepest longings of your heart. Praise Him for His provision, and pray to be reminded of this when you are faced with uncertainty and doubt.

Day 5: Defined by the Longings of Our Hearts

Read God's Word

Search me, God, and know my heart; test me and know my anxious thoughts. See if there is any offensive way in me, and lead me in the way everlasting.

Psalm 139:23-24

Reflect and Respond

A strong, sensitive, and independent young woman, Mary Katherine wants to be loved for who she is. She finds that she doesn't neatly fit into the mold that many women in her community embody; she wants to be loved and accepted for her own strengths, not just because she can be a good farm wife. When Jacob begins to show interest in her, Mary Katherine pushes him away, fearful that his love of farming would pull her into a life she doesn't want to lead.

Excerpt from Chapter 2

The little bell over the door tinkled as Mary Katherine entered the shop. She hurried to hang up her bonnet and coat. "I'm sorry I was gone so long."

"You weren't," her grandmother assured her. "And it's been slow."

"Did you have a good time with Jacob?" Anna asked, her eyes sparkling with mischief.

Mary Katherine stopped. "How do you know I bumped into Jacob?" She narrowed her eyes. "Or wasn't it an accident that I bumped into him?"

Shrugging, Anna pushed a needle through the quilt she was working on.

"Anna?"

She looked up, the picture of innocence. "Yes, Grossmudder*?"*

"Are you matchmaking?"

Anna blinked. "No, Grossmudder*."*

Mary Katherine moved to stand near Anna. She put her hands on her hips and gave her a stern look. "So our running into each other was a coincidence?"

"No." She knotted the thread and resumed sewing. "He asked what time we ate dinner each day, and I told him we ate at the shop but you liked to take a walk about noon each day."

"I see."

Anna's lips twitched, and then she started giggling. "I'm sorry. But I saw the two of you talking last Sunday and you seemed interested in him."

"Mary Katherine's interested in someone?" Naomi asked as she walked out of the supply room. "Here, can you help me with these bolts of fabric?"

Taking several of the bolts that were threatening to slip from Naomi's grasp, Mary Katherine carried them to the cutting table. Naomi began unfolding a bolt and pulled a pair of scissors from a drawer.

"I'm not interested in Jacob," Mary Katherine told Naomi. "I was polite. Nothing more."

"You were gone a long time." Anna glanced up and batted her eyelashes. "That must have been some walk."

Mary Katherine walked over to the window and looked out. "We ran into Daniel—" she stopped and looked at Anna.

"I haven't talked to Daniel," Anna said quickly.

Nodding, Mary Katherine glanced out the window again. "Daniel and Jacob hadn't eaten, so I sat with them and had some tea."

Frowning, she walked over to her loom, sat down, and placed her feet on the treadle. Picking up the shuttle, she ran her fingers over the smooth wood. She touched the fibers that were the color of the ocean and began weaving the shuttle in and out, back and forth, and felt peace settling over her as she sat in her favorite place in the world.

"You were with two *handsome men?"*

"Anna, enough teasing!" Leah said sternly.

"Yes, Grossmudder.*"*

Mary Katherine felt a hand on her shoulder and looked up.

"Are you allrecht, liebschen*?" her grandmother asked, her blue eyes filled with concern.*

"I'm fine." She looked over her design for a moment.

"Did Jacob say something to upset you?"

She shook her head.

"Daniel?"

She shook her head.

"Then—?"

"I'm sure they'll be very happy together," Mary Katherine muttered.

Naomi's scissors clattered to the table. "Are you saying that Jacob and Daniel uh—um, don't like women?" she stammered, and her face went as scarlet as a rotrieb.

Mary Katherine laughed, and then she sighed. "Nee. I doubt they think about women much. Farming *holds too much of their hearts."*

The bell over the door jingled merrily as someone opened it. Mary Katherine glanced over and was surprised to see Daniel and Jacob entering the shop.

Anna greeted Daniel with a smile and after speaking with him a moment, led him to a display of yarns. Mary Katherine remembered that he'd said he wanted to get a gift for his mother.

Jacob stood by the front counter and looked over at Mary Katherine with that intense look of his.

"He seems very interested in you," Leah murmured.

"It doesn't matter," Mary Katherine said, pulling her gaze from him and returning to her weaving. "I told you. He's in love with farming."

Leah stared at her, perplexed. "There's something wrong with farming? Your father is a farmer."

Then she paused. "Oh, I see the problem," she said slowly.

"Do you?" asked Mary Katherine. She stopped and stared at the multi-colored pattern on the loom before her, wishing she could find one for her own life. Lifting her gaze, she looked into her grandmother's eyes. "Do you?"

More than anything, Mary Katherine wants to feel understood—to know that someone understands her deepest desires and longings and fears and loves her anyway. How does her grandmother, Leah, show Mary Katherine that she is known and loved?

Is there someone in your life who "gets" you—who understands your hopes, desires, fears, and doubts? Who is that person, and how does he/she encourage and support you?

We are all like Mary Katherine—we all want to know that we are not alone, that we are understood and accepted, that we are loved, in spite of and because of all of the doubts, fears, hopes, and dreams that make us who we are.

In many ways, our lives are defined by the longings of our hearts, and if we are willing to take a brave look at how we respond to those longings, they will point us to the deepest desires of our hearts. If we long to be restored, we might pursue perfection here on Earth. If we long to be loved at all costs, we might be willing to morph into whatever form it takes to get love from someone else. If we long for peace, we might choose to fade into the background of our relationships, hoping not to cause any trouble or rock the boat. If we long for passion, we might search out things that give us a temporary thrill or excitement. If we long for acceptance, we might become workaholics to gain approval and appreciation.

Our hearts are complex places, and at times our longings can seem overwhelming and even consuming. But God Himself formed our hearts and our minds and gave us complex emotions and thoughts. The longings themselves are not bad; in fact, they are beautiful, for when we take a prayerful look at the

We are not alone…we are understood and accepted… we are loved, in spite of and because of all of the doubts, fears, hopes, and dreams that make us who we are.

deepest desires of our hearts, we find that everything our hearts long for can be found in God.

God can use the deepest longings and groanings of our hearts to point us back to Him and His love.

King David cried out, "Search me, God, and know my heart; test me and know my anxious thoughts. See if there is any offensive way in me, and lead me in the way everlasting" (Psalm 139:23-24). Take some time today to stop and name the deepest desires and longings of your heart. List them below.

God can use the deepest longings and groanings of our hearts to point us back to Him and His love.

Ask yourself how these desires are manifesting themselves in your life and how you are trying to fulfill them. Where are you turning for fulfillment?

Read the following verses. What does each have to say about how God meets the deepest desires of our hearts?

Ephesians 1:3-6

Zephaniah 3:17

God, our loving Creator, has given us life and brought us into His family. He has focused His love on us, adopted us, and given us indescribable mercy and grace, lavishing His love over us and delighting in us. How amazing to know that every desire of our hearts is fulfilled through Him!

Talk with God

Lord, open my eyes to all the blessings and gifts You have so graciously bestowed on me. Help me to have eyes to see that You are the hope and desire of my heart and that You alone can fulfill my deepest longings and desires. I praise You for your generous and reckless grace. Help me to live in that knowledge and to offer up all of my longings to You with open hands so that You can take those longings and fill me with more of You. Amen.

As You Go

Take some time to pray today over the longings and desires you identified. Ask God to speak His words over these longings and desires, and to give you assurances about each desire you've identified as having power in your life.

About the Amish

Who are the Amish?

The present-day Old Order Amish—often called the Plain people for their simple way of life and clothing—grew out of Swiss and Alsatian emigrants who traveled to the United States in the late 1600s after a schism within a group of Anabaptists in their homeland. Their leader was a man named Jakob Ammann (sometimes spelled Amman), and so they came to be known as the Amish.

In the eighteenth century, Amish and Mennonites (a group that split off from the Amish and that is less restrictive) settled in Pennsylvania, which today is the site of the second-largest number of Amish in the United States. Ohio is the largest. Today, there are over 273,000 Amish living in thirty U.S. states, according to the Young Center for Anabaptist and Pietist Studies at Elizabethtown College.[3] There also are Amish living in Canada.

Traditional Amish generally speak Pennsylvania German (Pennsylvania Dutch). Some Old Order Amish communities speak a dialect of Swiss German. While some Amish communities remain more isolated, others interact with the modern world, such as in Lancaster County, Pennsylvania. Here the Amish interact with their *Englisch* neighbors as well as the many people who visit their community from around the United States and the world.

What is the Amish way of life?

The Amish place a heavy emphasis on church and family. Church is the cornerstone of their life and community. A church district is usually composed of twenty to forty families who meet in a member's home on a rotating basis every other week. Each district is led by a bishop and several ministers and deacons. Every church member must follow the rules of the church, which are called the *Ordnung*. These rules govern daily living and include prohibitions or limitations on the use of electricity, telephones, automobiles, and clothing.

On the weeks when the community does not gather for Sunday services, the people spend time visiting friends and doing family activities. Homes are designed to accommodate large gatherings by having movable walls inside. Church benches travel on a large wagon for the services, which are usually three hours in length and conducted by lay ministers. A light lunch is served afterward. Social events include work "frolics" and singings.

The Amish become members of their church in their late teens and early twenties after being given a chance to experience life outside their community. Nearly 80 percent will choose to become baptized in the Amish faith because of the strong family and community bonds they've developed. Those who wish to marry must be baptized first. Once a person joins the church, he or she may marry only within the faith community. There is no divorce in the Amish community. An Amish family usually has an average of seven children, so the number of Amish is growing in the United States.

The Amish value rural life, hard work, humility, and privacy. While many *Englischers* (what the Amish call the non-Amish) are curious about the Amish, they prefer to keep to themselves, following 2 Corinthians 6:14: "Do not be yoked together with unbelievers. For what do righteousness and wickedness have in common? Or what fellowship can light have with darkness?"

Children attend school in the Amish community, usually in one-room schoolhouses. The Amish won this right to educate their young according to their religious beliefs after a court battle that reached the Supreme Court. After the children graduate from school in the eighth grade, they often are involved in apprenticeships and other learning opportunities and continue to help their families—working the farm, doing carpentry, and performing jobs in other businesses.

The Amish take care of their elderly and infirm and share the expense of medical bills. They pay taxes but generally do not collect Social Security. Being pacifists, they are exempt from military service. They do, however, practice their belief of helping outside the community by holding fundraisers for charitable causes, such as Haiti.[4]

What kind of rules do the Amish follow?

The *Ordnung* is a written and unwritten set of rules that governs Amish life. These rules include everything from how the Amish dress to how they run their personal and professional lives. The Amish were an agriculture-based community until recently. Now, with land soaring in value in Pennsylvania, the Amish often are involved in other types of work, sometimes conducting business in the *Englisch* community.

When at home, however, the Amish do not use electricity. Gas or propane is used for household appliances, and telephones are kept in a shanty outside. Some communities allow cell phones for business purposes only, while others look the other way for personal use as well. Some communities forbid them entirely. The main reason electricity is not used is because the Amish believe it is not conducive to family life. Television and radio would hinder the close relationships that come

from talking to one another and doing things together. The Amish also are not allowed to own automobiles. Horse-drawn buggies help to keep everyone close, as well as to prevent the Amish from the kind of "keeping up with the Joneses" that the *Englisch* practice.

The rules are strict: members who violate them are excommunicated, and shunning— avoiding members who do not conform—is still practiced in some areas. The shunning isn't punitive; rather, the Amish hope to convince the shunned member to come back to the flock.

Video Notes
A Few Minutes with Barbara

Interesting Insights:

Points I'd Like to Discuss with the Group:

Week 2
The Wounded Heart

Scripture for the Week

At that time Jesus declared, "I thank you, Father, Lord of heaven and earth, that you have hidden these things from the wise and understanding and revealed them to little children; yes, Father, for such was your gracious will. All things have been handed over to me by my Father, and no one knows the Son except the Father, and no one knows the Father except the Son and anyone to whom the Son chooses to reveal him. Come to me, all who labor and are heavy laden, and I will give you rest. Take my yoke upon you, and learn from me, for I am gentle and lowly in heart, and you will find rest for your souls. For my yoke is easy, and my burden is light."

Matthew 11:25-30 ESV

Setting the Stage

Life has a way of shaping us, and not always through the ways we would choose. The battlefields of our lives can leave us battered and scarred like an oft-tested warrior, weary from the fight. But out of the struggle comes triumph and a quiet knowledge that our scars can be beautiful reminders that there is a bigger story only God can tell. This week we will explore how our wounds can lead us to the Great Healer, and how learning to forgive as He does can lead us to a transformed life.

Excerpts from Chapters 3 and 6

Think you're too good to work on a farm, do you?
[Mary Katherine jerked her head up and glanced around. But she was alone in the room.]

No need to look up and around to see who spoke. She recognized the voice now. It was her father's. He'd chastised her for years for the way her teacher said she daydreamed in class, even though she'd overheard him saying he hadn't done well in schul himself.

But he had repeatedly criticized her for her for not liking work on the farm and seemed to dole out the most unpleasant chores to her, to the point where she'd stopped complaining.

Her grandmother had saved her by bringing her to work at Stitches in Time. . . .

The shop door swung open and shut so quickly the bell over it gave a funny clanging noise as a man stepped inside the shop.

Mary Katherine glanced up from her seat at her loom and her heart sank.

"Your grossmudder in the back?" he asked in a brusque tone.

She nodded and watched him walk toward the back of the store, then open the door and shut it firmly behind him. It took a couple of minutes before she could return to her work. Even then her hands shook, and she fumbled with the pattern and had to redo half an inch.

The store was so quiet she could hear the tick-tock of the clock. Or was it the beat of her heart?

The bell rang merrily again, and when Mary Katherine looked over, she saw Naomi and Anna stroll in, arm in arm, their faces lit with laughter.

They stopped when they saw Mary Katherine and rushed over.

"What is it? What's the matter?" Naomi asked, taking Mary Katherine's hand in hers.

"Did we get robbed?"

Naomi elbowed Anna. "Oh stop! You're such a drama queen!"

With her free hand, she pulled up a chair and sat beside Mary Katherine. "If we'd been robbed she wouldn't be sitting here at her loom. She'd be chasing the crook down the sidewalk."

"I wish I were as brave as you think I am," Mary Katherine said through stiff lips.

"Your hand is cold as ice. What's upsetting you?" Anna wanted to know as she drew a chair up on the other side of her cousin.

Before Mary Katherine could speak, the door leading to the rear of the store opened and the man strode out, giving them a stern glance as he walked to the door, and then, just as he was about to exit, he turned and looked back at Mary Katherine. He opened his mouth and then hesitated.

Scowling, he wrenched open the door, letting in a blast of cold air, then left, shutting the door behind him with a bang. The bell jangled from the wind and the movement.

Mary Katherine shivered and gathered her shawl closer around her shoulders.

"Well, and hello to you, too," Anna muttered.

"Don't be rude," Naomi told her.

"Me? He's the one who's rude. He didn't even stop to say a word to us!" Anna exclaimed, indignant. "Why does he have to act so unfriendly?"

Mary Katherine frowned. "How should I know? I think he's always been grumpy." She rubbed her cold hands and turned her attention to her loom.

"Didn't he come to talk to you?"

Swallowing at the lump in her throat, Mary Katherine shook he head.

Leah walked into the room, carrying a box. "Oh, good, you're back," she said to Naomi and Anna.

Then she glanced at Mary Katherine. "Did your dat leave already?"

"Ya."

"He didn't even say hello to us," Anna told her. She glanced at Mary Katherine, then at her grandmother. "I don't think he said a word to her."

Setting the box down on the counter next to the cash register, Leah crossed the room. "Is that true?"

Nodding, Mary Katherine kept her eyes on the steadily growing length of material in front of her. Focus on the waves, she told herself. Blue, blue, blue waves rolling out, rolling in. Peace. Serenity. Breathe in, breathe out.

Naomi, always sensitive to the moods of others, touched her arm. "So he said nothing to you?"

She shook her head. "He came to see Grossmudder." She couldn't look at her. If her grandmother wanted her to know why he'd come today—if her father had wanted her to know—one of them would have told her. So she stared at her weaving, determined not to let it hurt that he hadn't even acknowledged her.

"But you're his daughter," Anna declared. She put her hands on her hips. "Since when does a father walk by his daughter and not say a word?"

"He nodded," Mary Katherine said through stiff lips. She put down the shuttle and stood. "I'll be right back."

Her grandmother reached out to touch her arm, but Mary Katherine rushed past, slipped into the restroom, and shut the door.

She clutched at the cold porcelain sink and stared at her reflection in the mirror. "I am not going to cry. I am not going to cry." She didn't. But her lips quivered and she had to blink again and again.

"Mary Katherine?" her grandmother called through the door. "Are you allrecht?"

"I'm fine! I'll be right out!"

She tore off a section of paper towel, wet it with cool water, and pressed it to her cheeks. When she felt composed, she threw the towel in the wastepaper basket and opened the door.

Her grandmother stood there, her hands folded at her waist, and regarded her with sympathy. "I'm sorry that he hurt your heart."

Mary Katherine held up a hand. "I'm fine. Really. I know he's never going to change." She started to walk past her grandmother.

"And you?"

She stopped and turned. "Me? Why do I need to change?"

Leah tilted her head and studied her. "Just because he doesn't understand you doesn't mean you can't forgive him."

"You want me to forgive him." Her voice was flat.

"I want you to want to forgive him."

Mary Katherine laughed but the sound held no humor. "He turned his back on me when I wanted to come here and work at the shop."

"I know. But you can forgive someone who doesn't know better, can't you?"

"I tried," Mary Katherine whispered. "I tried."

"I know." Leah regarded her with kind eyes. "Sometimes it takes two people. Actually, most of the time it takes two."

"He'll never change," Mary Katherine blurted out.

"Never say never."

With that, she left the room, going out into the shop, leaving Mary Katherine to stand there staring after her.

Leah tilted her head and studied her. "Just because he doesn't understand you doesn't mean you can't forgive him."

Day 1: When We're Wounded

Read God's Word

"The LORD will fight for you, and you have only to be silent."

Exodus 14:14 ESV

Reflect and Respond

For as long as she can remember, Mary Katherine has experienced pain and rejection in her father's presence. Whether assaulted by his biting, scathing words or suffering through his disapproving silences, Mary Katherine's heart and spirit have been wounded by her father's actions and attitude. And though she finds peace and joy in being in her grandmother's home and shop, the weight of those wounds still affects the way she lives her life.

In William Faulkner's novel *Requiem for a Nun*, one of the characters says, "The past is never dead. It's not even past."[1] Doesn't that statement often feel true? Though we try to move past the wounds that life has given us, at times it seems our present is hijacked by our past, and we are once again consumed with the hurts and offenses that have shaped our lives.

In the introductory excerpt for this week, we see an interaction between Mary Katherine and her father. How does her father act toward Mary Katherine?

How does she react to seeing him?

What emotions do we see Mary Katherine experiencing?

We are all battle-weary warriors, and the weavings of our lives leave marks on us, big or small.

How does Mary Katherine try to deal with these emotions? Do you think she tries to avoid them or to deal with them head on?

We live in a fallen world, and all of us have been wounded in one way or another. We all carry the scars of living and of battles fought. Some of us have been shaped by dramatic, life-altering events, while others have been shaped in quieter, subtler ways. Nevertheless, we are all battle-weary warriors, and the weavings of our lives leave marks on us, big or small.

What do you think it means to be wounded by someone or something?

Think of a time when you have been wounded. What happened?

Have there been events or relationships in your life that have inflicted wounds upon your heart and spirit? How have they affected your life to this point?

How have you considered God in light of those events or relationships—have you believed He was present during those times, or distant? How has this affected your relationship with God?

Enslaved by the Egyptians for years, the beaten-down Israelites had suffered a cruel system of prejudice and marginalization under their masters. So when God sent Moses to lead them out of slavery, they were wary and afraid. But they followed Moses out of slavery in Egypt and into the desert and an unknown future. Their bravery did not last long, though, when they heard that Pharaoh and his army were pursuing them, and their resolve quickly dissolved into panic and fear.

> *When Pharaoh drew near, the people of Israel lifted up their eyes, and behold, the Egyptians were marching after them, and they feared greatly. And the people of Israel cried out to the LORD. They said to Moses, "Is it because there are no graves in Egypt that you have taken us away to die in the wilderness? What have you done to us in bringing us out of Egypt? Is not this what we said to you in Egypt: 'Leave us alone that we may serve the Egyptians'? For it would have been better for us to serve the Egyptians than to die in the wilderness." And Moses said to the people, "Fear not, stand firm, and see the salvation of the LORD, which he will work for you today. For the Egyptians whom you see today, you shall never see again. The LORD will fight for you, and you have only to be silent."*
>
> *The LORD said to Moses, "Why do you cry to me? Tell the people of Israel to go forward. Lift up your staff, and stretch out your hand over the sea and divide it, that the people of Israel may go through the sea on dry ground. And I will harden the hearts of the Egyptians so that they shall go in after them, and I will get glory over Pharaoh and all his host, his chariots, and his horsemen. And the Egyptians shall know that I am the LORD, when I have gotten glory over Pharaoh, his chariots, and his horsemen." . . .*

Then Moses stretched out his hand over the sea, and the LORD drove the sea back by a strong east wind all night and made the sea dry land, and the waters were divided. And the people of Israel went into the midst of the sea on dry ground, the waters being a wall to them on their right hand and on their left. The Egyptians pursued and went in after them into the midst of the sea, all Pharaoh's horses, his chariots, and his horsemen. And in the morning watch the LORD in the pillar of fire and of cloud looked down on the Egyptian forces and threw the Egyptian forces into a panic, clogging their chariot wheels so that they drove heavily. And the Egyptians said, "Let us flee from before Israel, for the LORD fights for them against the Egyptians."

Then the LORD said to Moses, "Stretch out your hand over the sea, that the water may come back upon the Egyptians, upon their chariots, and upon their horsemen." So Moses stretched out his hand over the sea, and the sea returned to its normal course when the morning appeared. And as the Egyptians fled into it, the LORD threw the Egyptians into the midst of the sea. The waters returned and covered the chariots and the horsemen; of all the host of Pharaoh that had followed them into the sea, not one of them remained. But the people of Israel walked on dry ground through the sea, the waters being a wall to them on their right hand and on their left.

Thus the LORD saved Israel that day from the hand of the Egyptians, and Israel saw the Egyptians dead on the seashore. Israel saw the great power that the LORD used against the Egyptians, so the people feared the LORD, and they believed in the Lord and in his servant Moses.

Exodus 14:10-18, 21-31 ESV

Whether or not we can feel Him, God is present in every battle of our lives, and He is fighting for us.

We face battles in this life, but we are not alone. Whether or not we can feel Him, God is present in every battle of our lives, and He is fighting for us. He did not abandon the Israelites, and He will not abandon us. He will fight for our hearts and for our healing. And He will win the battle.

How does it make you feel to consider that God is fighting for you? How does the Israelites' story in Exodus 14 encourage you?

Do you sense or see God fighting for healing in your life? If so, in what areas? How are you responding to Him?

Moses told the people, "The Lord will fight for you, and you have only to be silent" (Exodus 14:14 ESV). Why do you think he told them to be silent?

Talk to God

God, I ache from my wounds. They make me feel weak and helpless. And sometimes they make me wonder if You have abandoned me. But You promise to always be with me, Lord, and I can sense Your guiding hand in my life. I choose to believe that You are with me, fighting for me and making me whole. I believe, Lord. Thank You for Your persistence and mercy. Amen.

As You Go

Reflect today on how God might be fighting—working—in your life. Where is He asking you to be silent and let Him fight?

Day 2: He Will Carry Our Burdens

Read God's Word

"Come to me, all who labor and are heavy laden, and I will give you rest."

Matthew 11:28 ESV

Reflect and Respond

We all remember those formative childhood moments when we felt rejected, confused, or hurt by another person's actions: when your best friend decided she wanted to be best friends with someone else, when you were picked last for kickball, when you tripped and fell in front of the whole class en route to the blackboard and everyone laughed.

As we grew, so did the weight of those moments. Your first love—the guy you were sure was the one forever and ever—broke up with you and started dating someone else. You got waitlisted by your number-one college pick. The sorority you were hoping to pledge dropped you. The company you were dying to work for said you just weren't the "right fit."

I remember feeling very wounded when my father said he had not saved enough money to send both my brother and me to college and had decided to send my brother. He told me it was more important for the man to get an education because he was the one who would support a family. Well, I was shocked; I didn't know he felt that way. He said he'd pay for one year of nursing school. I didn't want to be a nurse.

I decided I would pay my own way, enrolled in the local community college (*not* in nursing classes), and went after a job at the local newspaper where I'd done a journalism mini-internship. I got an entry-level "go-fer" job, which led to a job as a reporter after completing college classes, which led to a career as a writer—one I never could have imagined would make me so happy.

God, my ultimate Father, had bigger plans for me than my earthly father did.

At some point or another, someone has made every one of us feel as if we were not good enough, pretty enough, smart enough, worthy enough, fill-in-the-blank enough. Some of those instances were probably more trivial, and we eventually laughed them off, while others may have been so serious that we have dealt with their repercussions for years. Either way, these incidents can make us feel unworthy of love and acceptance and lead us to make choices that cause us additional grief and harm.

John 8:2-11 tells the story of a woman caught in a desperate state:

> *At dawn [Jesus] appeared again in the temple courts, where all the people gathered around him, and he sat down to teach them. The teachers of the law and the Pharisees brought in a woman caught in adultery. They made her stand before the group and said to Jesus, "Teacher, this woman was caught in the act of adultery. In the Law Moses commanded us to stone such women. Now what do you say?" They were using this question as a trap, in order to have a basis for accusing him.*
>
> *But Jesus bent down and started to write on the ground with his finger. When they kept on questioning him, he straightened up and said to them, "Let any one of you who is without sin be the first to throw a stone at her." Again he stooped down and wrote on the ground.*
>
> *At this, those who heard began to go away one at a time, the older ones first, until only Jesus was left, with the woman still standing there. Jesus straightened up and asked her, "Woman, where are they? Has no one condemned you?"*

"No one, sir," she said.

"Then neither do I condemn you," Jesus declared. "Go now and leave your life of sin."

What is your initial reaction when you read this story? What emotions does it stir within you?

What do you imagine is this woman's story? How might she have found herself in this predicament?

How do you imagine she felt as she stood before Jesus?

We do not know this woman's name or how she looked or what her past was like, but we can only imagine how humiliated and worthless she must have felt as she stood before Jesus. Caught in the act of adultery, her shame must have run so deep that she could barely breathe. (Not to mention that she was facing a death sentence for her mistake.) We will never know what events, relationships, and experiences in this woman's life led her to make the choices she made. We will never know how her situation was manipulated and exploited for others' gain. What we do know is this: Jesus had compassion for her and offered her not condemnation, but love and freedom. He offered her a second chance at life.

What do you think Jesus wanted to teach everyone gathered there that day about forgiveness?

What do you think He wanted to show the woman about her worth?

Why do you think Jesus told her to go and leave her life of sin? How was He addressing her view of her identity?

Mary Katherine's *Englisch* friend, Jamie, finds herself in a hard situation when she thinks she might be pregnant with her boyfriend's baby. Jamie, like Mary Katherine, has experienced conflict with and rejection from her own father, and she is living on her own at a young age. Knowing this, how do you think Jamie's past might have influenced her present circumstances and the mistakes she has made?

As we see in John 8 and in countless places throughout the Gospels, Jesus offers grace and love for our hurting hearts and messy situations. When we are heavy with pain and guilt, when we can barely lift our heads to look Him in the eye, Jesus says to come to Him and He will carry our burdens.

Jesus offers grace and love for our hurting hearts and messy situations.

Reread Matthew 11:28 and write the verse below in your own words.

What would it mean for you to lay down your burdens and receive Jesus' rest? How would it change the way you live your life?

Talk to God

Jesus, thank You that You throw no stones but respond to us with a love that transforms and changes us from the inside out. Thank You for being my refuge and a safe place of healing for my wounded heart. Thank You for the incomparable freedom that You offer my soul. Help me to dive deep into that freedom today. Amen.

As You Go

In what area of your life do you need to claim Matthew 11:28 today?

Day 3: The Good Father

Read God's Word

"But while he was still a long way off, his father saw him and was filled with compassion for him; he ran to his son, threw his arms around him and kissed him."

Luke 15:20b

Reflect and Respond

The word *father* conjures up many different thoughts and emotions. When some people hear *father*, words such as *love*, *protection*, *gentleness*, and *strength* come to mind. For others, all they can think is *fear*, *abandonment*, *judgment*, *rejection*, and *pain*.

Mary Katherine's father, Isaac, was clearly the head of his family. And though he worked hard and provided for his family's basic needs, his emotional and spiritual leadership of his family was certainly lacking. His wife and daughter were diminished in his domineering presence, and their spirits suffered from his general displeasure and criticism.

Though Mary Katherine doesn't intend for her view of her earthly father to interfere with her perception of her heavenly Father, doubt and lack of trust are seeping into her relationship with God. She finds herself talking less and less to God, and though she still wants a relationship with Him, in some ways she feels abandoned by God because He didn't rescue her from her unhappy family situation when she was younger.

How do you think Mary Katherine's view of God has been affected by her relationship with her own father? Which of her father's characteristics might Mary Katherine be projecting onto God?

What words come to mind when you think of *father*?

How has your relationship with your earthly father shaped your life?

How has your relationship with your earthly father shaped your view of God?

It doesn't take more than a brief look at the local news or newspaper to see that there are many fathers who are not doing a good job of loving and caring for their children. We've all heard the stories; some of us have experienced them firsthand. That makes the picture of fatherhood that Jesus describes in Luke 15 even sweeter.

There was a man who had two sons. The younger one said to his father, "Father, give me my share of the estate." So he divided his property between them.

Not long after that, the younger son got together all he had, set off for a distant country and there squandered his wealth in wild living. After he had spent everything, there was a severe famine in that whole country, and he began to be in need. So he went and hired himself out to a citizen of that country, who sent him to his fields to feed pigs. He longed to fill his stomach with the pods that the pigs were eating, but no one gave him anything.

When he came to his senses, he said, "How many of my father's hired servants have food to spare, and here I am starving to death! I will set out and go back to my father and say to him: Father, I have sinned against heaven and against you. I am no longer worthy to be called your son; make me like one of your hired servants." So he got up and went to his father.

But while he was still a long way off, his father saw him and was filled with compassion for him; he ran to his son, threw his arms around him and kissed him.

The son said to him, "Father, I have sinned against heaven and against

you. I am no longer worthy to be called your son."

But the father said to his servants, "Quick! Bring the best robe and put it on him. Put a ring on his finger and sandals on his feet. Bring the fattened calf and kill it. Let's have a feast and celebrate. For this son of mine was dead and is alive again; he was lost and is found." So they began to celebrate.

Meanwhile, the older son was in the field. When he came near the house, he heard music and dancing. So he called one of the servants and asked him what was going on. "Your brother has come," he replied, "and your father has killed the fattened calf because he has him back safe and sound."

The older brother became angry and refused to go in. So his father went out and pleaded with him. But he answered his father, "Look! All these years I've been slaving for you and never disobeyed your orders. Yet you never gave me even a young goat so I could celebrate with my friends. But when this son of yours who has squandered your property with prostitutes comes home, you kill the fattened calf for him!"

"My son," the father said, "you are always with me, and everything I have is yours. But we had to celebrate and be glad, because this brother of yours was dead and is alive again; he was lost and is found."

Luke 15:11-32

In this story we see the remarkable picture of a humble, loving father and how he responded in a gut-wrenching situation. His youngest son had tired of living in his father's house and wanted to go out into the world to live his own life. In those days, a son asking for his inheritance was basically saying to his father, "Why should I wait until you're dead to get my money?" It was a shameful, embarrassing situation for the family to have such a disrespectful and irresponsible son.

But when the son recklessly squandered what he'd been given and was forced to return to his father, the story takes an unexpected turn. His father looks out over the fields and sees a lone figure limping toward home. Maybe he had been watching, waiting expectantly for his son's return all along. But when he finally sees him, he starts running toward his disrespectful, ungrateful son. He *runs*. This is not the posture of a prideful man intending on punishing one who had shamed him. This is not the posture of a man who has had his feelings hurt and plans on turning a cold shoulder. This is the posture of grace.

Why do you think Jesus told this parable? What was He trying to say to those who were listening that day?

What is He saying to you through this story?

The father runs to his son and embraces him, eager to restore this prodigal and give him more than he could ever dare to ask for. This is a picture of our God. This is a picture of our Father. How sweet to know that God is the Good Father, committed to our restoration. He is not proud or self-protecting. He is not wounded or vindictive.

God our Father heals and protects. He embraces and rejoices. He guides with love and mercy. He offers us redemption, freely and completely.

Talk to God

Father, I am overwhelmed by Your perfect love for me. Open my eyes to who You really are, God, and how You want to care for me and give me life. Forgive me for thinking that I have You all figured out. Thank You for reassuring me that I can trust You with my heart and life and know that You will give me all good things. Thank You for adopting me as Your child. I am chosen. Amen.

God is the Good Father, committed to our restoration.

As You Go

Psalm 147:3 says, "He heals the brokenhearted and binds up their wounds" (ESV). How is this a picture of God the Good Father? Reflect on this today.

Day 4: Respect and Forgiveness

Read God's Word

Children, do what your parents tell you. This is only right. "Honor your father and mother" is the first commandment that has a promise

attached to it, namely, "so you will live well and have a long life." Fathers, don't exasperate your children by coming down hard on them. Take them by the hand and lead them in the way of the Master.

Ephesians 6:1-4 *THE MESSAGE*

Reflect and Respond

Our families represent the baselines of our lives, the starting points from which we gain understanding and experience about the world and other people. From them we are taught to have a certain perspective and to accept basic fundamentals about how life should be lived and how other people should be treated. Mary Katherine's early life experiences in her own family taught her that being a child (and being a female) landed her firmly in the place of being a second-class citizen and that her value depended on what she could do for her family.

As Mary Katherine grew and her perspective expanded a bit, she began to question her parents' example and the way her father treated her and her mother, Miriam. Receiving encouragement and kind guidance from other parental figures, such as her grandmother, Leah, Mary Katherine soon found that her view of the world did not match up with her parents' view of the world, and she chose to escape their home for an environment that encouraged her natural talents and abilities. Though Mary Katherine left her parents' home, she soon found out that she couldn't totally escape the effect their attitudes had had upon her life, and so we find her struggling with doubt, fear, and insecurity about her future.

How would you describe your relationship with your parents? What baseline for living life did you receive from them?

When Mary Katherine and her father, Isaac, do not see eye to eye, he often quotes Exodus 20:12 to her: "Honour thy father and thy mother: that thy days may be long upon the land which the LORD thy God giveth thee" (KJV). Why do you think he quotes this verse to his daughter? What do you think is his perspective on this verse?

Do you think this perspective is correct? Why or why not?

The same command appears again in Ephesians 6:1-3: "Children, do what your parents tell you. This is only right. 'Honor your father and mother' is the first commandment that has a promise attached to it, namely, 'so you will live well and have a long life'" (*THE MESSAGE*). Why do you think God gives us this commandment twice in the Bible?

Read the following translations of Ephesians 6:4.

*"Fathers, do not provoke your children to anger by the way you treat them. Rather, bring them up with the discipline and instruction that comes from the Lord." (*NLT*)*

*"Fathers, don't exasperate your children by coming down hard on them. Take them by the hand and lead them in the way of the Master." (*THE MESSAGE*)*

What are some examples of things parents might do to anger or exasperate their children?

Why is it significant that both of these commands—*Honor your father and mother* and *don't exasperate your children*—are included in the Bible? What do they point both parents and children to do?

> We are to love and respect each other not because we always deserve it, but because God commands us to love as He loves.

No parent who has ever walked the Earth has been perfect; likewise, there are no perfect children. We are all sinful, imperfect beings who like to live life on our own terms, and we will make mistakes—and make them often. That is why God encourages us to love and respect these people who play such a huge role in our lives. We are to love and respect each other not because we always deserve it, but because God commands us to love as He loves.

Likewise, God calls us to forgive. When Leah tells Mary Katherine that she needs to forgive her father for his words and attitudes, Mary Katherine is surprised that her grandmother would suggest she be the one to offer forgiveness. After all

the hurt he has caused Mary Katherine, she can't imagine that offering forgiveness to her father will change their relationship or his attitude.

As a child, it's easy to blame your parent for anything that you consider to be a failing. Maybe there was a time that you felt a parent didn't give you enough love or acceptance, or at least didn't show it when you needed it. But then when you become a parent yourself, you see how impossible a job it is—that you can't be everything for that child, and that most of the time you don't know what you're doing anyway.

Sometimes we forget that our parents did not emerge from the womb as the people they are today. They, too, have been shaped by the events and relationships in their lives, and they have their own scars to prove it. And though it can be hard to have compassion and see them as complete people and not just our parents, perhaps that is just the kind of gentleness that God asks us to extend to them.

The writer Oscar Wilde once wrote, "Children begin by loving their parents; after a time they judge them; rarely, if ever, do they forgive them."[2] In what ways do you identify with this statement?

How might choosing to live with a spirit of forgiveness toward her father—which involves learning to love him as he is, with all his own baggage and failings—change the way Mary Katherine sees him?

How can looking to God for love and acceptance play an important part in changing Mary Katherine's view of her father?

Talk to God

Heavenly Father, You alone are the source of true love and acceptance—not my parents, my family, or my own standards. Help me to remember this, Lord, and to love the people You have placed in my life with Your spirit of mercy and forgiveness. Help me to love. Help me to forgive. Help me to be gentle. Help me to reflect You. Amen.

As You Go

Galatians 5:22-23 says, **"But the fruit of the Spirit is love, joy, peace, forbearance, kindness, goodness, faithfulness, gentleness and self-control."** How can you apply these verses to your relationships with your family today?

Day 5: The Power of Words

Read God's Word

Let no corrupting talk come out of your mouths, but only such as is good for building up, as fits the occasion, that it may give grace to those who hear.

Ephesians 4:29 ESV

Reflect and Respond

We cannot escape the power of words. Written or spoken, whispered or yelled, words have the power to heal, destroy, encourage, and change. No matter the language, words have the power to affect our lives like little else.

Consider the life-changing power of these words:

Marry me.
I love you.
It's a girl! / It's a boy!
It's over.
I'm leaving.
Don't give up.
You'll never make it.
I believe in you.

I remember seeing a neighbor walking her dog in her front yard one evening. Even from across the street it was very obvious that something was terribly wrong. Her shoulders were slumped as if she carried the weight of the world on them, and

> Written or spoken, whispered or yelled, words have the power to heal, destroy, encourage, and change.

although she was only in her forties and physically fit, that day she moved like an old, arthritic woman.

I walked across the street and asked what was wrong. "Bill was told he has lung cancer today. You know the survival rates on that."

Well, I did, but I also knew my dentist had had those words spoken to him as well. And yet after an enormous, faith-filled fight, he is alive and well today.

I told her about him that day and insisted on talking to her husband. I called and asked my dentist if he would please bear witness about finding other words to help with the fight against cancer. The two men talked. Their wives talked. All of them prayed. Bill, a man who had to see things to believe them, let himself be talked into positive visualization.

Soon, different words were being spoken to Bill: "The tumor is shrinking." "We don't see any tumor." "You're now in remission."

Words. They changed an outlook that saw imminent death to one that believed in healing and life.

What words have you heard spoken that have changed your life?

"Gracious words are a honey-comb, sweet to the soul and a healing to the bones."
Proverbs 16:24
NIV

Over and over again, the Bible speaks about the power of words in our lives.

Read the following verses and write what each has to say about words.

Proverbs 29:20

Proverbs 16:24

Psalm 55:21

Colossians 3:8

Spoken words are so important because they seep into our hearts and minds, comprising the voices of encouragement or judgment that we hear over and over again in our minds.

The words of Mary Katherine's father have worn grooves into her mind over the years, and the voice that says she will never be good enough seeps into her thoughts, filling her with doubt that she will ever be a suitable wife for a good Amish man.

Excerpt from Chapter 5

[Mary Katherine] wanted to get married one day. Far into the distance. Maybe a couple decades from now. When she felt like she'd know for sure not to marry someone as autocratic as her father—a man who wouldn't try to crush the creativity out of her. After all, her grossmudder *had found one. Surely there had to be one that God had set aside for her. Someday. Somewhere.*

Schur, said a cynical little inner voice.

Schur.

Sometimes the voices inside our heads that whisper lies can often cloud the truths that God wants to speak into our lives. Hear the words the Lord speaks over you:

> *"For I know the plans I have for you," declares the LORD, "plans to prosper you and not to harm you, plans to give you hope and a future. Then you will call on me and come and pray to me, and I will listen to you. You will seek me and find me when you seek me with all your heart."*
>
> Jeremiah 29:11-13

> *[Jesus said,] "Do not let your hearts be troubled. You believe in God; believe also in me. My Father's house has many rooms; if that were not so, would I have told you that I am going there to prepare a place for you? And if I go and prepare a place for you, I will come back and take you to be with me that you also may be where I am.'"*
>
> John 14:1-3

> *"I have told you these things, so that in me you may have peace. In this world you will have trouble. But take heart! I have overcome the world."*
>
> John 16:33

Sometimes the voices inside our heads that whisper lies can often cloud the truths that God wants to speak into our lives.

"Never will I leave you; never will I forsake you."

Hebrews 13:5b

Which of these Scriptures speaks most clearly to your heart today? How is God speaking to you through its words?

God's words speak truth, peace, and hope into our wounded hearts, assuring us that He will always be with us. But sometimes it's hard to hear God's words over the constant clang and clatter in our lives, and that is when the encouragement of others becomes so important.

Though Mary Katherine sometimes hears the negative voice of her father in her life, she also hears words of encouragement from others who surround her. Why are these encouraging words so important in Mary Katherine's life?

Read Ephesians 4:29. How does God instruct us to use the words we speak to others?

Talk to God

Dear God, let Your words of love and hope wash over me today, reminding me of what is true. When the lies seep into my mind and threaten my peace, help me to recall Your words and remember that Your voice is the only one I need to hear. Amen.

As You Go

Write the words of Jeremiah 29:11-13 on a note card, in your planner, or on something else that you can carry with you today. Stop often during the day to read God's words to you, reminding you of whose you are.

Sometimes it's hard to hear God's words over the constant clang and clatter in our lives, and that is when the encouragement of others becomes so important.

About the Amish

Why is family so important to the Amish?

The Amish believe that children are a gift from God, so they hold the family as precious and God-centered. An Amish family puts one another above the distractions of the world. They show how important family is by having meals together without the distractions of the *Englisch* world (television, radio, and so on). They go to church together—church being a religious service held every other week in the home of a church member. And they host wholesome activities such as singings and athletic activities like volleyball at their homes. Families take care of one another. If there is a family farm, it is often taken over by one of the adult children, and the parents live in a separate apartment called a *dawdi haus* to be cared for if they need it.

What are family dynamics like in the typical Amish family?

The Amish family is large; seven is the average number of children. Older children help take care of younger siblings and help the parents in every way that they can. Amish children are taught respect and responsibility and traditional values. Every Amish child has chores and does not feel the need to ask for an allowance.

Amish families are traditional. Husbands carry the primary responsibility for providing for the family, while wives devote themselves to running the household and caring for the children. Girls learn how to do many household tasks from their mothers, and boys learn how to do the things done by their fathers, such as farming, home and farm maintenance, and caring for the family horse and buggy. However, there also is sharing of roles, particularly if the family runs a farm. Oftentimes wives and daughters help in the barn, fields, and shop, and husbands and boys help with the garden or chores around the house.

In some cases, women may own a business and provide a significant portion of the family income. Women with young children, however, seldom work full time outside the home, though some might run at-home stores or bakeries.

Men serve as the spiritual leaders of the home, though mothers are also very involved in nurturing the spiritual lives of their children. All religious matters pertaining to the church or outside world fall to the husband.

Extended families provide a sense of identity and a strong network of support within Amish communities. Adult sisters may get together once a month for a day of fun and work, enjoying time together and doing chores such as harvesting vegetables, cleaning house, or making quilts. Family members help one another at all times, especially when there is an emergency or death.

Video Notes
A Few Minutes with Barbara

Interesting Insights:

Points I'd Like to Discuss with the Group:

Week 3
The Insecure Heart

Scripture for the Week

"Come, all you who are thirsty, come to the waters; and you who have no money, come, buy and eat! Come, buy wine and milk without money and without cost.

Why spend money on what is not bread, and your labor on what does not satisfy? Listen, listen to me, and eat what is good, and you will delight in the richest of fare.

Give ear and come to me; listen, that you may live. I will make an everlasting covenant with you, my faithful love promised to David. . . ."

Seek the LORD while he may be found; call on him while he is near.

Let the wicked forsake their ways and the unrighteous their thoughts. Let them turn to the LORD, and he will have mercy on them, and to our God, for he will freely pardon.

"For my thoughts are not your thoughts, neither are your ways my ways," declares the LORD.

"As the heavens are higher than the earth, so are my ways higher than your ways and my thoughts than your thoughts.

As the rain and the snow come down from heaven, and do not return to it without watering the earth and making it bud and flourish, so that it yields seed for the sower and bread for the eater, so is my word that goes out from my mouth: It will not return to me empty, but will accomplish what I desire and achieve the purpose for which I sent it.

You will go out in joy and be led forth in peace; the mountains and hills will burst into song before you, and all the trees of the field will clap their hands.

Instead of the thornbush will grow the juniper, and instead of briers the myrtle will grow. This will be for the LORD's renown, for an everlasting sign, that will endure forever."

Isaiah 55

Setting the Stage

Though we sing hymns about God's powerful and complete love for us, and we quote Scriptures about His unending grace, if we are honest, we must admit that often our insecurities and fears overwhelm us and keep us from understanding and claiming just how much we are loved by God. So we try harder, and harder still, until we are defeated, exhausted, and hopeless. It seems that we can never do enough or be enough. The good news? God is enough.

This week we will look into our hearts (and our schedules) to see where we are misplacing our identities and our hopes in things that cannot satisfy, and we will learn how God fulfills the greatest desires of our hearts.

Excerpt from Chapter 6

A customer walked in, an Englisch *one, and smiled at her. Mary Katherine returned her smile.*

"Can I help you with anything?"

"I'd like to browse a little if you don't mind."

"Of course. Let me know if I can be of any help," Mary Katherine told her.

A glance through the shop window showed few shoppers out. No wonder. It had been drizzling since early morning. Her grandmother and her cousins were doing inventory, leaving Mary Katherine in charge.

The woman walked around the shop, studying the quilts displayed on the walls, especially the collage quilt Mary Katherine had made.

Mary Katherine walked over to her loom and studied her pattern.

"Are you Mary Katherine?"

She looked up at the customer. "Yes."

"Jamie told me about you. Jamie Patterson. She said I should stop by your shop. I'm Allie Prentice, one of Jamie's college instructors."

She studied Mary Katherine's work on the loom. "This is lovely. Quite a creative use of pattern and color. Where did you learn to do this?"

"An aunt of mine taught me years ago."

"Could I get you to come in and talk to my class about your weaving?"

Shocked, Mary Katherine stared at her. "I—I wouldn't know what to say. I just . . . weave."

"And quilt," the woman said, gesturing at the collage quilt. "I love the images, the unusual quality to it. I haven't seen many examples of collage quilts. I'd like you to talk about both to my Fabric Arts class."

"Jamie let me see her textbook for that class," Mary Katherine said, excitement welling up in her. "It looks so interesting."

The woman smiled. "Why don't you come in and speak, and then you can observe the class a few times if you like?"

"Observe?"

"Sit in, see what we do. You don't have to pay. Or take the quizzes," she added with a smile.

Mary Katherine hesitated. "When is the class?"

"Ten to eleven a.m. on Tuesdays and Thursdays." She pulled a business card from her purse and handed it to her. "Think about it and let me know what day is best for you. Oh, and I can send a driver to pick you up and bring you back."

She looked at the card in her hand, then at the woman. "I'll think about it and let you know."

"Great." The woman glanced at the clock on the wall. "Well, much as I'd like to browse for hours in here, I need to get back to campus. I have a ton of work to do."

Her grandmother came out a little while later. "Still quiet out here?" She peered at Mary Katherine. "You look a little flushed. Are you feeling allrecht?"

She still didn't know what to think of the visitor who'd walked out the door just a few minutes ago. "Wait until you hear who came in." . . .

She told her grandmother about the professor and how she wanted her to speak to the class.

"I don't know why she thinks I have anything important to tell the students," Mary Katherine said.

"Will you hide your light beneath a bushel?" Leah asked her quietly. "Child, I know that we teach—we live—working at not being filled with hochmut, with pride. But it's not prideful to share yourself and what you know with others, liebschen. You're not bragging about yourself, about your God-given gift, are you?"

Mary Katherine shook her head. "Never."

"And I've never known you to be self-important. As a matter of fact—"

"What?"

Leah sighed and reached out to touch Mary Katherine's cheek. "I love [your father], but he is not an easy man to be around. You've blossomed here."

Unbearably touched, Mary Katherine hugged her. "Danki," she whispered. "I was miserable on the farm."

"It wasn't the farm, it was—"

Conversation ceased as Naomi and Anna entered. They stopped when they saw their grandmother embracing Mary Katherine.

"Is everything all right?" Naomi asked, looking concerned.

"It's fine," Leah rushed to say. She stepped back from Mary Katherine. "Why don't you tell them your news while I make us some tea?"

> "I don't know why she thinks I have anything important to tell the students," Mary Katherine said.
> "Will you hide your light beneath a bushel?" Leah asked her quietly.

Day 1: Searching for Worth

Read God's Word

"Come, all you who are thirsty, come to the waters. . . . Why spend money on what is not bread, and your labor on what does not satisfy? Listen, listen to me, and eat what is good, and you will delight in the richest of fare."

Isaiah 55:1-2

Reflect and Respond

We are hungry and looking for something to fill us up, but we choose the wrong things, and we're left wanting soon after.

Recent days have seen a surge in the popularity of the local farmer's market. Every week in cities across the country, people gather at open-air markets to peruse the fruits and vegetables of many farmers' labor. It's amazing to see the variety, color, and richness of so much lovingly tended produce, and to know that the products you're buying are of top-notch quality and filled with rich nutrients for your body.

Imagine if you saw someone sitting on a bench just outside these amazing fresh produce stands chowing down on a cheap, greasy fast-food hamburger. The scene wouldn't make much sense. Why would someone pass up all the amazing, fresh, nutrient-rich foods in the stalls for something that will ultimately deplete the body and leave him or her hungry an hour later?

Yet often our lives mirror this scene. We are hungry and looking for something to fill us up, but we choose the wrong things, and we're left wanting soon after. Often we look for our love and self-worth in places that can't support the weight of our desires—we look to our relationships to give us love. We look to our careers to give us purpose. We look to our life roles (daughter, wife, mother) to give us identity. We look to our homes to give us safety. We look to our communities for acceptance. Any time we look for validation and love outside of God's love for us, we are eating the fast-food hamburger and passing up the fresh veggies—and our hunger won't be satisfied.

All of us struggle with looking to other things to define us and give us worth. From what you know about Mary Katherine thus far, how does she struggle with identity and self-worth?

To what or to whom does she look for validation?

If you are reading the novel, in what ways do other characters struggle with identity and self-worth? (Consider Jacob, Jamie, Naomi, and Mary Katherine's parents.)

Like Mary Katherine, many of us have struggled at some point in our lives with issues related to identity and self-worth. With the cultural messages and pressures we face as women today, most of us have questioned at one time or another whether we measure up. We find ourselves thinking that we should do more or be more. The mythical list of what we *should* be doing seems never ending. No wonder even the most self-assured of us sometimes question ourselves and our abilities!

When we find ourselves discouraged or disappointed, perhaps our problem is not that we need more *self*-esteem, but rather that we need to be filled with *God*-esteem—something beyond anything we can attain on our own. A first step is to take a close look at *where* we're investing ourselves—and to what benefit.

In Isaiah 55:2, God gives us some clues to find out where we are placing our hope and our search for identity. He says, "Why spend money on what is not bread, and your labor on what does not satisfy?" Based on this verse, what do "money" and "labor" represent in our lives?

In what areas are you currently spending your "money" and "labor"?

All of the things we tend to invest our lives in—our families, work, relationships, communities—are *good things*. They are certainly worth our time and attention, and God can use us to spread His love in these areas. But if we are looking to these things to give us worth and identity, they will fall short. They cannot satisfy our deepest desires. Our search will be never ending—and frustrating—if we try to find our identity and worth in these things.

Are you thirsty for more? Is your deepest hunger unsatisfied?

When you consider where you are placing your time, energy, resources, and expectations (also known as your "money" and your "labor"), what conclusions can you draw about where you tend to find your identity?

How are your relationships affected by the weight of expectations you are placing on them? Are they suffering? If so, how is God leading you to make some changes?

Talk to God

God, thank You for peeling back the layers of my desires to help me see where I put my hopes and expectations. Forgive me for looking to things other than You to fulfill the deepest desires of my heart. Open my eyes, Lord, and help me to see where I am misplacing my hope. Help me to let go of those people or things and to turn to You. Amen.

As You Go

Meditate today on Isaiah 55:2:

"Why spend money on what is not bread, and your labor on what does not satisfy? Listen, listen to me, and eat what is good, and you will delight in the richest of fare."

How can you turn from what does not satisfy and, instead, eat what is good?

Day 2: You Can't Earn Your Worth

Read God's Word

"Come, all you who are thirsty, come to the waters; and you who have no money, come, buy and eat! Come, buy wine and milk without money and without cost."

Isaiah 55:1

Reflect and Respond

Have you ever gone to a store and tried to buy something with no money? It's not likely that scenario worked out in your favor. Our whole economic system is based on currency—exchanging money for goods. This is a system that we understand from a very young age and adhere to throughout our lives. It's just the way things are done.

So, what does God mean when He says, "You who have no money, come, buy and eat! Come, buy wine and milk without money and without cost" (Isaiah 55:1)? What is He trying to tell us?

God, speaking through the prophet Isaiah, invites anyone who is thirsty or hungry to come to "the waters" and be satisfied. Throughout his book, Isaiah often describes God's kingdom and salvation in terms of an abundance of water, and the images of wine and milk represent symbols of complete satisfaction and comfort. He beckons us to come freely and partake without any way to pay. Titus 3:5 says, "[God] saved us, not because of righteous things we had done, but because of his mercy. He saved us through the washing of rebirth and renewal by the Holy Spirit."

When it comes to our salvation, fulfillment, and identity as children of God, we have entered the store with no money. There is no currency—wealth, abilities, strengths, good works—we can offer that could buy our redeemed status. Our precious worth was graciously bought on our behalf by Jesus' sacrifice and given to us by God. We must simply accept the gift.

Have you ever felt that you had to earn God's favor? If so, how?

> Our precious worth was graciously bought on our behalf by Jesus' sacrifice and given to us by God.

What do these verses say about that? Write your thoughts below.

Since we've compiled this long and sorry record as sinners (both us and them) and proved that we are utterly incapable of living the glorious lives God wills for us, God did it for us. Out of sheer generosity he put us in right standing with himself. A pure gift. He got us out of the mess we're in and restored us to where he always wanted us to be. And he did it by means of Jesus Christ.

Romans 3:23-24 *THE MESSAGE*

For many years, Mary Katherine has been frustrated in her efforts to earn her father's affection and favor. Do you think that struggle has influenced how she feels about God and earning His favor? If so, how?

How can you identify with her struggles?

In Luke 18, Jesus tells this story of a taxman and a Pharisee:

[Jesus] told his next story to some who were complacently pleased with themselves over their moral performance and looked down their noses at the common people: "Two men went up to the Temple to pray, one a Pharisee, the other a tax man. The Pharisee posed and prayed like this: 'Oh, God, I thank you that I am not like other people—robbers, crooks, adulterers, or, heaven forbid, like this tax man. I fast twice a week and tithe on all my income.'

"Meanwhile the tax man, slumped in the shadows, his face in his hands, not daring to look up, said, 'God, give mercy. Forgive me, a sinner.'"

Jesus commented, "This tax man, not the other, went home made right with God." (vv. 9-14a THE MESSAGE)

The people in the crowd who heard this story would have been shocked at Jesus' words. In their eyes, the two men described here certainly would have been

on different playing fields. Surely the taxman, a public servant who collected taxes and was notoriously deceitful (think of an IRS agent going rogue and pocketing your money), couldn't begin to accept God's favor, much less be more right with God than the Pharisee (the Scripture-soaked religious leader)!

But Jesus said it was so. The taxman's belief that God alone was enough—and that his own efforts could never measure up—is the correct view of God's love for us. Instead of working, striving, and posturing to get God's favor—and viewing ourselves as worthy to receive that favor—we must realize that it's not about us. God alone is the source of true acceptance, and we must learn to see ourselves as He see us: whole, pure, lovely, and perfect because of Christ's sacrifice. We cannot add to or take anything away from that. Instead, we can rest, knowing that no matter what we do, we are loved by the One who can fill our hearts and satisfy us completely.

Put yourself in the shoes of those who heard Jesus speak that day about the taxman and the Pharisee. How do you think you might have reacted to what He said? What would you have thought?

Take a few minutes to reflect on these words by poet Macrina Wiederkehr:

O God
help me believe
the truth about myself—
no matter how beautiful it is![1]

What do you think she is saying? How do her words encourage and challenge you?

How does believing the beautiful truth of God's gift of love and grace speak to your sense of self-worth?

> God alone is the source of true acceptance, and we must learn to see ourselves as He see us: whole, pure, lovely, and perfect because of Christ's sacrifice.

Talk to God

Heavenly Father, You alone have the power to save. You alone have the power to make me whole and complete. Thank You for doing the work, Lord. Help me to believe in Christ's sacrifice to make me perfect and complete in Your eyes. Thank You for loving and embracing me and giving me the identity of Your child. Help me to believe in this beautiful truth, Lord, and to cling to it when I feel lacking. You are the source of my worth, Lord, and I praise You for that gift. Amen.

As You Go

As you go about your day today, pray that God would reveal to you the ways in which you try to "earn" your worth and favor in His eyes. Pray He would give you eyes to see, and to remind you how He sees you.

Day 3: Fearfully and Wonderfully Made

Read God's Word

For you formed my inward parts; you knitted me together in my mother's womb. I praise you, for I am fearfully and wonderfully made. Wonderful are your works; my soul knows it very well.

Psalm 139:13-14 ESV

Reflect and Respond

The early Christian church in Corinth had its issues, just as our modern-day churches do. We don't know all the ins and outs of their struggles, but Paul's first letter to them gives us some insight into their struggles. As the Corinthian church struggled to find its way, members were apparently becoming imbalanced in some of their thinking—namely that those who spoke in tongues were more exalted or spiritual than those who didn't.

Read 1 Corinthians 12. Do you feel that there are spiritual gifts that are "less honorable" than others (vv. 22-24)?

What are your particular gifts and strengths? How do you feel about them?

How have others in the church responded to your gifts in the past? Have you received encouragement for those gifts, or have you felt that your gifts were inferior to others?

How has the response of others affected how you use your gifts?

As members of the body of Christ, we each play a vital role in God's work here on Earth. Though we tend to compare ourselves to others and try to "measure up" to determine our worth, there is sweet relief and reassurance in knowing that God has created each of us with specific and individualized gifts, strengths, and skills, and that He wants us to use them in service to the church and one another.

Reread Psalm 139:13-14. How does it make you feel to know that God has created every inch of your personality—that your gifts, strengths, and weaknesses were hand-crafted for you alone?

What frustrates you about your gifts?

What excites you about them?

There is sweet relief and reassurance in knowing that God has created each of us with specific and individualized gifts, strengths, and skills.

Though Mary Katherine hasn't found much support from her parents for her weaving, God slowly begins to show her how she can use her abilities to weave and teach to touch other people's lives.

Excerpt from Chapter 3

The bell jangled as the door opened.

Mary Katherine smiled as a little girl who looked to be about six came to stand by her and stare at her loom.

"Sally, don't bother the lady."

"It's no bother," Mary Katherine told the child's mother. She continued sending her shuttle in and out of the warp she'd set up on the loom.

The little girl watched, rapt. Mary Katherine smiled at her.

"Would you like to try it?"

Sally nodded. Mary Katherine lifted her to sit on her lap, gave her the shuttle, and helped guide it through the colored strands. She worked the treadle and enjoyed how excited the child became as she learned how to weave.

"That's a beautiful piece you're making," the other woman said. "How long does it take to make?"

They chatted until Sally complained that her hands were tired. Her mother lifted her from Mary Katherine's lap and set her on her feet.

"I'm not through shopping yet," she warned her daughter.

"I have just the thing," Mary Katherine said. She walked to a display, found the small wooden potholder frames one of her male cousins carved, and invited Sally to sit at a child-sized table so she could demonstrate how to use it.

"Have you ever made a potholder?" she asked Sally.

"I'm not sure she knows what one is," her mother confessed, looking embarrassed. "I don't cook much."

Mary Katherine didn't know how anyone managed to get by without cooking— or why they would want to—but she pulled out the plastic bag of fabric loops and strung them on the loom.

Sally looked at the box. "Aunt Betty has one of these things. She uses them to keep from getting burned when she gets something out of the oven."

"That's right," Mary Katherine agreed, and she smiled. "They're good whether you use a regular oven or a microwave."

Sally's forehead puckered. "You don't use microwaves, right? Because you don't have 'lectricity?"

"That's right. Here, now you try weaving one of these loops through this way."

Sally watched, and then she took a loop and performed the same action, biting her bottom lip as she concentrated on what she was doing.

The woman smiled when she looked up. "You're so good with her." . . .

"Look what I did!" Sally exclaimed, showing Mary Katherine how she'd woven the potholder.

"Almost done," Mary Katherine said with a smile. She showed Sally how to finish off the edges of the potholder and watched as the child did it with great absorption.

"I made it all by myself!" Sally exclaimed, then she looked at Mary Katherine. "Well, almost by myself. You helped."

"It turned out so pretty," Mary Katherine told her. . . .

"Thank you, lady, I had fun," Sally told her.

Her mother beamed at her daughter and nodded her approval.

In what ways do you think Mary Katherine could use her gifts to encourage her community?

Are you using your gifts to serve God by serving others? Why or why not?

Spend some time thinking about how God may be leading you to share your gifts with your community. Are you following His leading in those areas? How can you be more sensitive to His leading?

Talk to God

Lord, thank You for creating me so carefully and considerately. Thank You for gifting me with the ability to love and serve You. Help me to trust that You have created me with a purpose and have a vision for my life. Help me to rest in that love and purpose and to give of myself as You lead and guide me. Amen.

As You Go

Read Psalm 139 in its entirety today, meditating on the words and letting God speak to you of His love through them.

Day 4: Accepting God's Love

Read God's Word

But you are a chosen race, a royal priesthood, a holy nation, a people for his own possession, that you may proclaim the excellencies of him who called you out of darkness into his marvelous light. Once you were not a people, but now you are God's people; once you had not received mercy, but now you have received mercy.

1 Peter 2:9-10 ESV

Reflect and Respond

It only takes a few minutes of watching one of the many reality shows on TV to discover that many people have lost all respect for themselves and others. All the drama, cattiness, insecurities, back-stabbing, and name-calling leave us enthralled and amazed, thinking *Who DOES that?* Though entertaining, we are thankful that this level of drama exists on our TV channels and not in our own lives.

But perhaps the producers of these shows are on to something: what these people exhibit so dramatically on the screen is actually happening on a smaller scale in our own lives and hearts. Often we, too, are filled with distrust for others and are insecure about our own worthiness, making us apt to lash out at others, harbor unforgiveness, and hand out disapproval when threatened or provoked. Even though our lives generally are quieter, plainer, and less dramatic than those on TV, we secretly identify with their rash behavior.

I remember a time when I was insecure about my own worthiness. I was a stay-at-home mom and started writing fiction with the hope that I could continue to be at home with my kids instead of having to return to my job at the newspaper.

I went through rejection after rejection from editors and was beginning to feel that I'd never sell my writing.

So I entered a local writing contest with an article about a local historical figure. I thought I had a good chance with that. A second contest involved writing a poem about that historical figure. I loved poetry but didn't think I could write a poem—one that would win. A particularly critical high school English teacher's comments had left me feeling I had no talent in that area. She was so hyper-critical that many of us cringed when we walked into her classroom. Today I might wonder if she was that way because she didn't feel good about herself and her own talents. Back then—and for a long time after—I just absorbed that criticism and rejection.

Eventually I decided I had nothing to lose by writing the poem, and I might even win something. Who knew how many other writers would enter—or write what the judges would like. So I entered, and I tied for first place with a woman whose published poetry was very popular. The prize money paid for the outfit I sewed to attend the awards banquet, a haircut, and dinner out for my family. I felt better about my writing after that—something I've learned to thank God for each day now. I've also learned to forgive those who are critical, recognizing that they have not accepted themselves for the wonderful creations of God they are.

When we are unable to accept God's love for us and to see ourselves as whole and redeemed in light of God's grace, we cannot truly love others as God wants us to love them. When we seek to earn our worthiness through our actions, accomplishments, acts of service, good words, or a strong work ethic, we are ignoring God's unconditional gift of grace and subjecting others to the unrealistic standards and demands we have come to rely on.

Having a right view of ourselves is critical if we are to love and appreciate the value and worth others have as children of God; without it, we can become judgmental, haughty, and unforgiving. Quickly we can become closed off in our relationships, unable to love and serve others freely and without fear.

> Having a right view of ourselves is critical if we are to love and appreciate the value and worth others have as children of God.

Based on the demeaning way that Isaac, Mary Katherine's father, treats other people, how do you think he views himself? Do you think he is able to accept God's unconditional love? Why or why not?

If you are reading the novel, what other characters in *Her Restless Heart* seem to struggle in some way with accepting God's unconditional love for them? How do their relationships reflect this struggle?

In what ways do you struggle with accepting God's love? How do your relationships reflect this struggle?

Though fear and insecurity are marks of the human race, God gives us a higher calling. Our Scripture for today reminds us,

> *But you are a chosen race, a royal priesthood, a holy nation, a people for his own possession, that you may proclaim the excellencies of him who called you out of darkness into his marvelous light. Once you were not a people, but now you are God's people; once you had not received mercy, but now you have received mercy.* (1 Peter 2:9-10 ESV).

When we accept God's grace and redemption for ourselves...we have new eyes to see those around us.

God has lavished mercy on us and has made us whole. Though our actions and our motivations will always be less than perfect, we are redeemed because of His great love for us. When we accept God's grace and redemption for ourselves, embracing that good and perfect and undeserved gift, we have new eyes to see those around us. We see that they are less than perfect and that God has redeemed them. We see them as worthy, because that is how God sees them. We become more patient, loving, and willing to share of ourselves. We celebrate one another, despite our grand imperfections, because God has celebrated us.

Read Mark 12:28-31. What do these verses call us to do—and in what order? Is this command difficult for you? Why or why not?

Read Zechariah 7:9. What does God command us to do in this verse?

Administer _____ _____; show _____ and _____ to one another. (NIV)

Now read Romans 9:14-16. According to these verses, what is "true justice"? What do these two verses together tell us about how we should treat other people?

What do each of the following verses have to say about how we should relate to others?

James 4:6

Romans 15:7

Matthew 18:21-22

Romans 12:16

1 Peter 3:8

To what standards do you tend to hold people accountable—your own standards or God's standards? How might God be leading you to change your perspective in this area?

How might Mary Katherine's perception of her father have changed sooner if she had fully embraced God's love and acceptance for herself?

Talk to God

Father, some days it is hard for me to believe that You have forgiven me completely and fully accepted me (with all my imperfections) into Your family. On those days, it's even harder to believe that You have done the same for those around me and that You love them just as unconditionally as You love me. Help me to realize that my fears and insecurities disappear in Your presence and that I don't have to live in their shadow anymore. Help me to love others as You love them and to see them as the beloved children they are. Amen.

As You Go

Reflect and meditate on 1 Peter 2:9-10. How does this verse affect your perspective today?

Each and every one of us has insecurities and fears that plague our hearts, and more often than not, we doubt ourselves and our abilities—sometimes to the point of stifling our hopes and dreams.

Day 5: The Importance of Community

Read God's Word

Two are better than one . . . for if they fall, one will lift up his fellow. But woe to him who is alone when he falls and has not another to lift him up! Again, if two lie together, they keep warm, but how can one keep warm alone?

Ecclesiastes 4:9-11 ESV

Reflect and Respond

Each and every one of us has insecurities and fears that plague our hearts, and more often than not, we doubt ourselves and our abilities—sometimes to the point of stifling our hopes and dreams.

Though the dominance of the Internet has had many negative effects on our culture, there are some ways in which it does foster community. Consider the blogosphere (as some affectionately call it), where ordinary women like you and me can voice our fears and insecurities and doubts and struggles and find community in others who understand what we are going through, reassuring us that we are not alone in our desire to lead fulfilling lives. Within this community of like-minded, gracious women, we can find comfort, solidarity, hope, and encouragement to continue the good fight.

While Mary Katherine doesn't exactly have access to a virtual community of supporters, she does find great support among the women in her life. Her grandmother, Leah; her cousins Naomi and Anna; and her friend Jamie all help Mary Katherine to realize that her insecurities and doubts don't have to define her; she can grow and flourish and celebrate the ways in which she is gifted. Their loving, encouraging words help to combat the negative, wounding words that filled her childhood and call her to dream big.

Excerpt from Chapter 6

Mary Katherine sat at the table in the back room, glumly studying her notes. What makes you think you can talk to a class? A college class? . . . .

"What's all this?" Naomi asked as she entered the back room of the shop.

Mary Katherine moved some of her papers so that Naomi could join her at the table.

"I'm making notes for my talk."

"Ah, yes, the talk. I'm sure you'll do a fine talk."

"I'm not so sure," Mary Katherine muttered, frowning at what she'd scribbled on index cards. "I'm no speaker."

"No," Naomi agreed. She held up her hand and smiled when her cousin jerked to attention. "But you're a natural-born teacher. I saw how you taught that little girl how to make a potholder one day. And you're always explaining to people how to weave when they stop and ask questions. I think you love it."

"I love to talk to people about what I love to do," Mary Katherine pointed out, meeting her cousin's gaze. "I don't know how many of the students in the fabric arts class are that interested in weaving."

"I'd imagine the professor wouldn't have asked you if she thought you'd bore her class. And they're students interested in making clothes and such. Some of them might be very interested."

Mary Katherine nodded. "I hope you're right. But if I see the students dozing off, I'm going to stop."

Naomi laughed. "Okay, I don't see that happening, but if they do, ya, I guess it'd be a good idea to turn the class back to the professor. I'm sure she'll know how to deal with it."

How do these women in Mary Katherine's life encourage her to release her insecurities and fears?

Do you have a community that does this for you? How do they support and encourage you?

Reread Ecclesiastes 4:9-11. How have you found the wisdom in these verses to be true?

We desperately need others in our lives to help us live in our strengths and combat our weaknesses. We need allies; we need family.

The relationship between Mary Katherine and her grandmother, Leah, illustrates a beautiful partnership much like the one described in the book of Ruth.

Ruth, a young widow, and Naomi, her mother-in-law, were facing a crisis. The men in the family had passed away. Naomi's husband and two sons, one of whom was married to Ruth, had died, and the women of the family were left with a tough decision about what to do next. In biblical times, being a single woman wasn't exactly a favorable option; women were often treated as second-class citizens and forced to depend solely on their husbands or male relatives for support and provision. With very little choice to make, Naomi decided she had to return to her family in Bethlehem.

We don't know much about Ruth and Naomi's relationship before this point, but what we do know is telling: Ruth chose to follow her mother-in-law, Naomi, home. Maybe their relationship had been great from the beginning; maybe they started out rocky and became closer over time. Regardless, Ruth trusted and loved Naomi enough to follow her to a strange land and a strange people. And Naomi loved Ruth enough to help her find a husband who would love and care for her. (You can read the rest of the story in Ruth 2–4.)

Like Ruth, Mary Katherine chose to follow her grandmother in her strong faith and gentle attitude, and, like Naomi, Leah brought her granddaughter into her home to love and nurture her.

Read Ruth 1:16-17. What do you imagine inspired Ruth to speak these strong, determined words? What must she have thought of Naomi and how Naomi treated her?

How does Leah thoughtfully provide an environment for Mary Katherine in which she can flourish?

Leah demonstrates great love and respect for Mary Katherine. When Mary Katherine comes into conflict with her parents yet again, feeling hurt and frustrated, Leah challenges her to discover where her identity truly is.

Excerpt from Chapter 12

Mary Katherine reached over to cover her grandmother's hand with hers. "It's the best thing that ever happened to me. The day you invited me to come work here, and to live with you."

Leah smiled. "It was a very good day for me, too." Her smile faded, and her expression grew troubled. "I wanted you to be happy, to do the kind of work you have such a talent for. But you're still restless, still . . . feeling unloved, aren't you?"

"I'm not—" Mary Katherine began.

But her grandmother's words rang true. So true. Her shoulders sagged as she acknowledged the truth.

Her grandmother reached to clasp her hands. "I'm sorry that your father never loved you the way you needed, and in her not speaking up you felt abandoned by your mother, too. But I think you're forgetting something, dear one. I think you're forgetting Whose child you are."

"I'm the child of Isaac and Miriam."

Leah smiled slightly. "You're God's child, dear one. If He loves you, how can you feel unloved?"

Like water falling onto parched soil, words of truth spoken in love can sink into our dry, thirsty hearts and revive us, pointing us to the One who knows all our

> Words of truth spoken in love can sink into our dry, thirsty hearts and revive us, pointing us to the One who knows all our hopes, fears, doubts, and desires and who shelters us and cares for us.

hopes, fears, doubts, and desires and who shelters us and cares for us. We need reminders about where our true identities lie because so easily we can become confused and distracted in our search for true fulfillment.

Read Ephesians 5:19-20. What do these verses tell us to do?

How is God using the words of truth spoken from others to heal your heart? Are you listening for His voice in the words of those who love you? What is He saying to you?

Talk to God

Heavenly Father, You alone know what I need to hear and how to answer my insecurities and fears. Open my ears so that I may hear You above all else—so that I may hear Your words of love, comfort, and acceptance and know that they are from You. Thank You for the peace, joy, and hope that Your presence brings. Use me to speak Your words to others. Amen.

As You Go

Who is God calling you to love on today? Ask God to direct you and give you the words that need to be spoken to another. Pray for the certainty and the boldness to speak His words over someone else today.

About the Amish

What is the Amish view of self-esteem? What do they think about individuality?

Often people say they don't think they could live like the Amish. They frequently mention that they love the idea of living a simple life and wish they could enjoy things the way the Amish do. But they acknowledge that they couldn't give up television, automobiles, and other modern conveniences—or their sense of individuality.

It is true that the Amish place less emphasis on individuality than the *Englisch* do. They dress alike and wear their hair in a similar fashion. They view the individual as *part* of the whole, rather than the whole. The whole means the greater collective, which has higher value than the individual.

The Amish find their identity in family and in living in community. They do not put themselves and their needs first but, rather, practice humility.

In Amish culture, words such as *materialistic, individualistic,* and *pleasure-seeking* are practically non-existent. They do not need or desire the modern conveniences and material goods that their *Englisch* neighbors might consider necessities. In fact, it is not their custom to do anything for self-gratification or self-indulgence. In all things they value practicality, simplicity, and self-denial over comfort and convenience, and they consider the common good more important than personal gain.

In a sense, the Amish show a high sense of self-esteem by living according to the spiritual way of life Jesus practiced: giving up one's self to a greater good—the community. They teach us that by transcending our self-interest and choosing to live for others as Jesus did, we are able to live the kind of life that God desires.

What do the Amish do for fun?

If you're wondering if the Amish know how to have fun, the answer is yes! However, their idea of what is fun might be different than what the *Englisch* often consider to be fun. For the Amish, often the boundary between work and leisure can be blurred. For example, working in the fields or preparing dinner might be fun to the Amish but seem more like drudgery to others.

There are many activities that the Amish enjoy participating in for fun and recreation. Here is a list of common pasttimes:

hunting
fishing
camping
birdwatching
sports
board games
card games
reading
sewing
letter writing
auctions
visiting (perhaps the most common leisure activity)

It is important to note that some of these activities may not be approved in some communities or churches, such as participation in sports in more conservative communities. Even so, the Amish view leisure time as a way to enjoy family and friends and rest from the busyness and work of everyday life. It serves as a way to refresh and renew themselves as well as to strengthen a sense of community.

Video Notes
A Few Minutes with Barbara

Interesting Insights:

Points I'd Like to Discuss with the Group:

Week 4
The Reluctant Heart

Scripture for the Week

While Paul was waiting for [Silas and Timothy] in Athens, he was greatly distressed to see that the city was full of idols. So he reasoned in the synagogue with both Jews and God-fearing Greeks, as well as in the marketplace day by day with those who happened to be there. A group of Epicurean and Stoic philosophers began to debate with him. Some of them asked, "What is this babbler trying to say?" Others remarked, "He seems to be advocating foreign gods." They said this because Paul was preaching the good news about Jesus and the resurrection. Then they took him and brought him to a meeting of the Areopagus, where they said to him, "May we know what this new teaching is that you are presenting? You are bringing some strange ideas to our ears, and we would like to know what they mean." (All the Athenians and the foreigners who lived there spent their time doing nothing but talking about and listening to the latest ideas.)

Paul then stood up in the meeting of the Areopagus and said: "People of Athens! I see that in every way you are very religious. For as I walked around and looked carefully at your objects of worship, I even found an altar with this inscription: TO AN UNKNOWN GOD. *So you are ignorant of the very thing you worship —and this is what I am going to proclaim to you.*

"The God who made the world and everything in it is the Lord of heaven and earth and does not live in temples built by human hands. And he is not served by human hands, as if he needed anything. Rather, he himself gives everyone life and breath and everything else.

"From one man he made all the nations, that they should inhabit the whole earth; and he marked out their appointed times in history and the boundaries of their lands. God did this so that they would seek him and perhaps reach out for him and find him, though he is not far from any one of us. 'For in him we live and move and have our being.' As some of your own poets have said, 'We are his offspring.'"

Acts 17:16-28

Setting the Stage

Decisions have a way of resting heavily on our shoulders. When it comes time to make the big calls, we are often reluctant—hesitant, frozen in indecision, fearful that we will make the wrong choice, afraid that our hearts and minds will betray us and lead us down a path from which we will not recover. When we find ourselves weak, weary, and worn out from the battles that rage within, we need only turn to God, our Creator and Father, Who is never far away. As Paul states in Acts 17:28, "For in him we live and move and have our being." This week we will discover how God plays a very active role in our lives, and how we can live confidently and boldly, knowing that He is in control.

Excerpt from Chapter 6

"Jenny!" Mary Katherine smiled at her cousin Matthew's wife.

"Am I interrupting?" Jenny gestured at the note cards.

"Nee, come on in." She gathered up the cards, bound them with a rubber band, and set them aside.

Jenny placed the folder she carried on the table, then walked to the stove. She held up a mug, asking Mary Katherine if she wanted more tea before pouring some for herself and coming over to sit down.

[Jenny had] been a ghost of the woman she was now when she came here to Paradise to live with her grandmother. The bombing that had ripped at her body had scarred her soul as well, Mary Katherine knew. But as she renewed her relationship with Matthew—they'd fallen in love as teenagers here but been yanked apart by her father—Jenny had healed emotionally as well as physically. She had married Matthew, and just a few years ago, had even experienced what many thought was one of God's miracles when she had a baby.

She carried a quiet contentment now, a serenity and inner spirit of joy that was more than physical beauty. Mary Katherine envied—just a little—that surety of purpose Jenny carried. Inside, Mary Katherine felt like a big jumble of questions and indecision.

"How's Gabriel?"

Jenny beamed and her gray eyes sparkled. "Such a happy kind. *It's hard to believe he's one year old already." She glanced at the folder she had placed on the table. "Thought I'd work while Hannah teaches her class. As long as I'm not bothering you?"*

"No, I was just taking a break to work on something for a few minutes." . . . "Can I ask you something?" Mary Katherine blurted out.

"Sure."

"I heard you used to work on television when you were Englisch, before you joined the Amish church. You were a reporter?"

"Yes, I remember those days well." She glanced down at her Plain clothes and smiled ruefully. "I bet people would really be surprised at how I look now. On the other hand, so many people are fascinated by the Amish these days . . ." her voice trailed off, and she became lost in thought.

She shook her head. "I'm sorry, I got sidetracked there for a minute. I guess I really need some caffeine to stay awake today. I was up late last night—the book deadline looms. Anyway, you asked me about being on television?"

"Were you ever nervous?"

Jenny laughed. "Oh, my, yes! I didn't ever think of myself as a reporter. I just wanted to get the story out about how children were being affected by war overseas. Are you making notes for a talk?" she asked, glancing at the index cards.

Mary Katherine looked at them and shivered. "This professor wants me to talk about my weaving to her class. I can't imagine talking to a lot of people."

"I never thought about how many people might be listening to me," Jenny told her seriously. "That would have scared me to death. I just talked to one person— the cameraman."

"But you had an important message." Mary Katherine got up and paced around the room. "You were passionate about it, and for good reason. It's not like I have some great purpose here with my talk."

"You're passionate about weaving, and for good reason. You're good at it, you're creative, and the things you create help someone make their home a warmer, brighter place."

Jenny tilted her head. "Look, I don't want to talk badly about your father, but I hear things and I wonder if your self-esteem isn't suffering a little from all his criticism."

Self-esteem? That wasn't a term used often in the Plain community. Mary Katherine barely knew what it was. She knew she felt bad when he criticized her, and here, in the shop, she felt free and appreciated—and not just because the occasional customer admired her work or even bought it.

"The class probably won't be expecting you to be some practiced speaker," Jenny pointed out. "They'll appreciate hearing how you learned, how you work."

Mary Katherine acknowledged that with a nod and returned to sit at the table. . . .

Getting to her feet, she picked up Jenny's cup, warmed it up with more hot coffee, and set it before her. . . . "Jenny?"

"Yes?"

She bit her lip and lifted her eyes to meet Jenny's. "May I ask you something?"

"Sure."

"I'm used to seeing Plain people leaving—"

"But not an Englischer *like me—or Chris—coming to stay?" Jenny smiled and nodded.*

"Ya. And you seem happy here. Even with all the rules. The lack of things like a computer to write with," she said, waving her hand at the notepad in front of Jenny.

"Well, I always liked writing by hand, but I know what you mean. It seems backward to you for me to leave what I had and move here. But you see, things weren't important to me. I met this man and his three children, and we became a family. And then along came another special little someone and, well . . . what more could I want?"

Jenny reached out and touched Mary Katherine's hand. "I'm not suggesting that all you have to do is meet the right man and everything will be fine. You have to know who you are and what you want first. I know you still don't know if joining the church and living here is right for you. Only you can decide that. Well, you and God."

Mary Katherine felt a stab of embarrassment. She hadn't talked to Him much lately. She'd felt He had left her, had abandoned her to live unhappily with her earthly father.

She glanced at the clock and rose. Unlike her father, her grandmother never watched the clock and treated her like a slave. "I'd better get back to work. It was so nice to talk to you."

Impulsively, she bent down to hug Jenny. "Thanks."

"I know you're struggling," Jenny told her quietly as she returned the hug. "I've been there. Once you trust Him, you'll have the answers to your questions about where you belong."

"I hope so."

"Mary Katherine?"

"Yes?"

"You seem so happy since you came to work here. I think God had such a good plan for you with living at your grandmother's and working here at the shop with her and your cousins, don't you? Can you have that somewhere else?"

Mary Katherine found herself thinking about what Jenny had said as she worked in the shop the rest of the afternoon. She was tired of being in limbo, of feeling she was living a temporary existence, caught between two worlds.

Was it possible she wasn't seeing this last year as a sign that God had indeed been thinking of her, making a plan, looking to help her create a happy future?

Day 1: Making Decisions

Read God's Word

"The God who made the world and everything in it is the Lord of heaven and earth and does not live in temples built by human hands. And he is not served by human hands, as if he needed anything. Rather, he himself gives everyone life and breath and everything else.

"From one man he made all the nations, that they should inhabit the whole earth; and he marked out their appointed times in history and the boundaries of their lands. God did this so that they would seek him and perhaps reach out for him and find him, though he is not far from any one of us. 'For in him we live and move and have our being.' As some of your own poets have said, 'We are his offspring.'"

Acts 17:24-28

Reflect and Respond

Each and every day we are forced to make countless decisions. Some of them are small, with small consequences: What should I eat for breakfast? Which drycleaner should I use? Should I go to the grocery store now or wait until later this afternoon? Will my son want the blue shorts or red shorts washed for soccer practice? Others are bigger decisions, with potentially far-reaching effects: How should I discipline my daughter for sneaking out last night? Which school will be best for my kids? Should I even consider that new job offer when I'm content in my current position? When is the best time to talk with my husband about the fight we had last night?

When it comes to making decisions, some of us are up to the task. We love taking decisive action and moving on, ready for the next step. We say, "Let's do it. Let's go for it!" Meanwhile, others of us are slow to decide, overly cautious and wary of making decisions. Instead of committing, we tend to defer to other people, hoping that they will have more knowledge and courage to make the tough calls.

Different personalities react differently when called upon to make decisions. Which camp do you tend to fit in? Circle one:

**I easily   I am slow to commit
make decisions.   when making decisions.**

Why do you think you react the way you do?

What are the benefits and drawbacks of being quick to make decisions?

What are the benefits and drawbacks of being slow to make decisions?

To what extent do you think God should factor into your decision making?

That's a key question, isn't it? Do you believe that God belongs in your decision making? It's an interesting question to ask, because most of us Christians would say, "Yes, of course God belongs in our decision making." But to what extent do we really believe that to be true? Some people seem to believe that God should weigh in with a yes or no on every little decision in their lives; others feel that, if we are believers in the work Jesus did for us on the cross and have the Holy Spirit inside of us, God already exists in everything that we do and every decision that we make. Perhaps the better question is, If you are a Christian, why *wouldn't* God factor into your decision making?

Reread today's Scripture passage, Acts 17:24-28. What does each verse have to say about God's authority and power in each of our lives?

Verse 24

Verse 25

Verse 26

Verse 27

Verse 28

After reading and studying this passage, what do you think is the correct posture we should have before God—at all times, and especially when making decisions? Circle one answer. (Hint: check out 2 Chronicles 7:14.)

Fear
Humility
Insecurity

When it comes to making tough decisions in our lives, it's natural for us to feel afraid. It's normal to be reluctant when making big commitments. It's common to feel that we must make the *right* decision, and that making the wrong one will cause our lives to spin recklessly out of control or lead us down paths we don't want.

Mary Katherine is facing some big life decisions, including whether or not to embrace her Amish faith and recognize Jacob as the man she should marry and build a life with. Why do you think she is reluctant to make these decisions?

"If my people, who are called by my name, will humble themselves and pray and seek my face and turn from their wicked ways, then I will hear from heaven, and I will forgive their sin and will heal their land."
2 Chronicles 7:14

Laboring over making a tough decision can break us down and make us weary and confused. Like Mary Katherine, we can worry that maybe we've missed God's will for our lives or misinterpreted what He's trying to tell us. We can easily reach a place where we become insecure and doubtful, wondering if God is silent—or worse, absent.

What decisions are you struggling with today?

Are you opening yourself to God in making these decisions? If so, how? If not, why not?

What hopes and fears are wrapped up in these decisions? How is your heart faring?

Talk to God

God, if I am honest, I will admit that I don't trust You enough with the decisions in my life. Too often I rely on my own understanding and logic to make decisions and choices, but I want Your guidance in my life. I know that You have created me for a certain plan and purpose, and that You are the guide for my life. Help me to seek You and to know Your will. Amen.

As You Go

Today, reflect on Matthew 6:9-13, where Jesus instructs us how to pray (see below). How does praying this prayer put your heart and mind in a state that is open to hearing God?

> *[Jesus said,] "This, then, is how you should pray:*
> *'Our Father in heaven, hallowed be your name,*
> *your kingdom come, your will be done, on earth as it is in heaven.*

Give us today our daily bread.
And forgive us our debts, as we also have forgiven our debtors.
And lead us not into temptation, but deliver us from the evil one.'"

Day 2: Trusting God to Guide Your Steps

Read God's Word

It was just before the Passover Festival. Jesus knew that the hour had come for him to leave this world and go to the Father. Having loved his own who were in the world, he loved them to the end. . . . [Jesus said,] "Do not let your hearts be troubled. You believe in God; believe also in me. My Father's house has many rooms; if that were not so, would I have told you that I am going there to prepare a place for you? And if I go and prepare a place for you, I will come back and take you to be with me that you also may be where I am. You know the way to the place where I am going."

Thomas said to him, "Lord, we don't know where you are going, so how can we know the way?"

Jesus answered, "I am the way and the truth and the life. No one comes to the Father except through me. If you really know me, you will know my Father as well. From now on, you do know him and have seen him. . . . If you love me, keep my commands. And I will ask the Father, and he will give you another advocate to help you and be with you forever—the Spirit of truth. The world cannot accept him, because it neither sees him nor knows him. But you know him, for he lives with you and will be in you. I will not leave you as orphans; I will come to you. Before long, the world will not see me anymore, but you will see me. Because I live, you also will live. On that day you will realize that I am in my Father, and you are in me, and I am in you. Whoever has my commands and keeps them is the one who loves me. The one who loves me will be loved by my Father, and I too will love them and show myself to them. . . .

"All this I have spoken while still with you. But the Advocate, the Holy Spirit, whom the Father will send in my name, will teach you all things and will remind you of everything I have said to you. Peace I leave with you; my peace I give you. I do not give to you as the world gives. Do not let your hearts be troubled and do not be afraid."

John 13:1; 14:1-7, 15-21, 25-27

Reflect and Respond

It was Passover, a night of celebrating God's provision for His people. Jesus and His disciples sat at a dimly lit table. The mood was somber. He had just revealed to them that He would be leaving them, that His time on Earth was short-lived. Sad and confused, the disciples wondered what they would do when Jesus left. Where would they go? How would they carry on?

Certainly Jesus spoke gently, softly: "Do not let your hearts be troubled. I will not leave you as orphans; I will come to you." Though the disciples had been in the actual presence of God in the form of His Son, Jesus, they came unhinged as uncertainties about their futures and their ministry began to overwhelm them. Though they had seen Jesus perform miracles with their own eyes and experienced His gentle leading, they still had a hard time wrapping their minds around what it takes to truly follow Jesus: trust.

Reflect on today's Scripture reading. Imagine yourself in the sandals of these twelve disciples for a moment. What thoughts might have gone through your mind?

What would have made you afraid?

What would have made you hopeful? Which words of Jesus would have comforted you the most?

Do you find it hard to trust God at times? In what ways?

Jesus said, "Peace I leave with you; my peace I give you. I do not give to you as the world gives" (v. 27a). What promises of peace does this world offer us, and how is God's peace different?

The old hymn says, "Trust and obey, for there's no other way / To be happy in Jesus, but to trust and obey." The Old Testament is filled with stories of God asking His people to trust Him, to believe that He had everything under control and all they had to do was listen and obey, even if the road seemed impossible.

Consider the story of Noah. Perhaps one of the best-loved stories in the Bible, the story of Noah and the ark is pretty outrageous when you stop to think about it. When God spoke to Noah and told him to build a massive boat, what must have gone through Noah's mind? Did he think he was going crazy? And what about his family? Can you imagine what it would have taken for them to get on board with the idea?

It must have seemed like an insane situation, and yet Genesis 6:22 says, "Noah did everything just as God commanded him." Noah had a decision to make: to obey God even though he didn't understand fully where the outcome would take him, or not to obey and to follow his own wisdom instead. After all, the Bible says that Noah was "a righteous man, blameless among the people of his time, and he walked faithfully with God" (Genesis 6:9). Noah was wise, knowledgeable, and fair. He obviously had many good qualities that would allow him to make intelligent decisions on his own. What if Noah had chosen to rely on his own wisdom and decided that he must have misunderstood God, that it was an absurd idea to build a boat bigger than anyone of that time had ever seen? What would have been the effect of his disobedience and lack of trust? All of mankind would have suffered. But he trusted and obeyed, and God's will was done.

Have you ever taken a leap of faith and followed God's leading, even though you were unsure about how things would turn out? What happened?

In order to make the best decision for our lives, we must choose to trust that God's ways are higher than ours, and that only He can make the impossible perfect.

Jesus told the disciples that, though He was leaving them in body, He was not leaving them alone: "But the Advocate, the Holy Spirit, whom the Father will send in my name, will teach you all things and will remind you of everything I have said to you" (John 14:26). And the same is true for us. Though we have never felt Jesus' physical touch or heard Him speak to the restless crowds, He is with us nonetheless, and we can trust that the Holy Spirit leads us and directs our steps. Though we may never fully understand His ways, we can choose to trust in His Word and His love for us, and we can choose to obey. In order to make the best decision for our lives, we must choose to trust that God's ways are higher than ours, and that only He can make the impossible perfect.

Talk to God

Lord Jesus, I am so grateful that You sent the Holy Spirit to live in my heart and to guide my steps. I'm so grateful that I don't have to rely on my own understanding, and that I can trust You with every aspect of my life. Help me to do that. Help me to act confidently in faith and walk in obedience, knowing that I can trust You. Amen.

As You Go

What is going on in your decision making today? Are you being indecisive? Are you making hasty decisions? Today, trust God to guide your steps as you confidently move forward.

Day 3: Understanding What God Asks of Us

Read God's Word

He has shown you, O man, what is good; and what does the LORD require of you but to do justly, to love mercy, and to walk humbly with your God?

Micah 6:8 NKJV

Reflect and Respond

As evidenced by your desire to participate in this study, it's likely that you have already made the life-changing decision to embrace the gospel of Jesus Christ and have committed your heart and life to Him. Now you are committed to growing in your faith and intimacy with God.

How did you come to know God's unconditional love and grace for you? Briefly tell the story of your faith journey.

For many of us, trusting God with our hearts is the easy part—it's what comes after that seems so complicated. Our minds are flooded with questions: Which church should I join? Where does God want me to serve? What should I change about my life? Does God want me to sell everything I have and move to Africa? Am I serving Him in the "right" way? Sometimes we get so caught up in trying to serve God in the *right* ways that we tend to miss the big picture.

Micah 6:8 says, "He has shown you, O man, what *is* good; and what does the Lord require of you but to do justly, to love mercy, and to walk humbly with your God?" (NKJV). God doesn't ask us to try harder or work harder in order to win His approval and love. We don't earn or win His approval at all. All God asks of us is to walk in intimate relationship with Him and to love and care for others. All the other details will sort themselves out as He makes our paths clear, including those places where He wants us to serve using our God-given gifts and talents.

As Mary Katherine struggles in her decision to join the church, she asks for advice from her friend Jenny, an *Englisch* outsider who chose to join the Amish community. What are your thoughts on Jenny's choice to join and marry *into* the Amish community and faith?

> For many of us, trusting God with our hearts is the easy part—it's what comes after that seems so complicated.

Have you ever struggled with the decision to join a church? If so, what made that decision difficult for you?

What did you decide to do? How did you find God leading you through that process?

The total commitment of the Amish to their faith and way of life cannot be denied. In every aspect of their lives, seven days a week, they are committed to living out the things they believe to be true. Though many of us admire their devotion and commitment, we are likely overwhelmed when we think about making that kind of total-life commitment ourselves. The countercultural ways of the Amish emphasize community and family, and being a part of their culture demands that members look beyond their own needs and desires and devote themselves to caring for one another. Their commitment to community is deep and strong.

Are you currently committed to a particular church or community of believers? If so, why did you choose to commit to these other believers? If not, what are the obstacles you've faced in that area, or what is holding you back from making a commitment?

We need one another to encourage us in God's promises and to remind us of our status as dearly loved children of God.

Though we all belong to the global community of believers, it is important to develop relationships with other believers in our communities and churches. We need one another to encourage us in God's promises and to remind us of our status as dearly loved children of God. It's vitally important—and it's not always easy.

Growing in intimacy with others demands a lot of us; it means that we must be willing to risk being vulnerable and authentic. It demands that we put aside our reluctance and fear and believe that, as children of God who are *already* fully loved and accepted by our heavenly Father, we can be exactly whom He has created us to be. We don't have to hide in the shadows of our imperfections and shortcomings, but we can step into the light of His grace to fully love and accept others and be the community of believers God calls us to be. We don't have to put the pressure on our communities to define us, because we have already been defined by our state as forgiven, loved children of God.

This knowledge frees us to love others and serve where God leads us, without fear or regret, knowing that our lives are in His hands. The pressure to make all the *right* decisions is off!

In what ways do you struggle to give yourself fully to your community? Have you ever struggled with wanting (or not wanting) to be defined by your church or community?

Read Hebrews 10:19-25. How does what Jesus has already done for you allow you to live within the community of believers? How can this knowledge change your perspective on church/community?

Talk to God

Jesus, You have done the work of restoring me and bringing me into right standing with God. Because of Your love and sacrifice, I am defined by two words alone: God's child. As I interact with other believers, help me to remember that they, too, carry this label, and that we are all fully loved and accepted in You. Help me to throw off my insecurities and fears about being vulnerable and authentic with others so that I can wholeheartedly join together with other believers to do Your work here on earth. Amen.

As You Go

Today, take some time alone with God and ask Him to reveal to you the ways in which He wants you to grow in your relationships with other believers. How can you open yourself up to loving and serving others?

Day 4: Saying Yes to Things with Eternal Value

Read God's Word

As Jesus and his disciples were on their way, he came to a village where a woman named Martha opened her home to him. She had a sister called Mary, who sat at the Lord's feet listening to what he said. But Martha was distracted by all the preparations that had to be made. She came to him and asked, "Lord, don't you care that my sister has left me to do the work by myself? Tell her to help me!"

"Martha, Martha," the Lord answered, "you are worried and upset about many things, but few things are needed—or indeed only one. Mary has chosen what is better, and it will not be taken away from her."

Luke 10:38-42

Reflect and Respond

"Hi, friend! How are you?"

"Oh, hey! I'm so sorry I haven't called you back yet. I've just had a crazy week, and I feel like I've barely had two seconds to myself all day. How about you? . . . What have you been up to?"

"Oh, the same. Between the kids' school projects and work, I'm just fried. And my house is a total wreck right now. But we're doing fine . . ."

Does this conversation sound familiar to you? Do you ever feel burned out, distracted, and suffering from a debilitating case of the "to dos"? Do you collapse into bed at the end of each day, realizing that you have spent very little time with the people you love, let alone in God's presence? Are you tired? Exhausted, maybe? Maybe it's time to step back and take a closer look at what's driving you.

Think about how you've spent your time in the last twenty-four hours. What areas (or what people) claimed most of your time?

Are you happy with the way your time was spent? Why or why not? Can you identify an area in which you might need to make a change?

Instead of reluctantly doing everything we *think* we should be doing every day, what if we have the courage to step back and say, *Wait a minute—is this the right thing?* Believe it or not, God cares about how we spend our time, energy, and resources. Consider Jesus' encounter with Mary and Martha in Luke 10.

The realities of life often demand that there are certain things we must do, whether we want to or not. Eating is one of those things. As mothers know all too well, we need to eat, and we need to do it at least three times a day, which takes

Instead of reluctantly doing everything we *think* we should be doing every day, what if we have the courage to step back and say, *Wait a minute—is this the right thing?*

a lot of time, energy, and effort if you are trying to avoid making drive thrus a regular part of your menu.

In this story we see Martha in the kitchen, frantically trying to prepare for her guests. Who could blame her? It was a *big* deal to have Jesus show up at your house. Any of us would have done the same. When a large group—including a local celebrity—shows up at your house, there are things that need to be done. So when Martha got frustrated and flustered, Jesus spoke to her kindly. "Martha, it's okay. Stop for a minute. Come and sit with me."

Martha wasn't doing anything bad; in fact, she was probably playing into her natural strengths of organization and hosting. And Jesus wasn't chastising or patronizing her; He just wanted her to know that she didn't have to find her identity in being the best cook, hostess, or housekeeper in the village. Jesus just wanted her to know that she was enough in His presence, and that she could set aside her work and rest in that knowledge.

In what areas of your life are you spending your time and energy because you think those things define who you are and give you worth?

After reflecting on Martha's story, what do you hear God saying to you about those things?

More often than not, we women tend to make decisions about where to spend our time and resources based on everyone else's needs but our own. How does the story of Mary and Martha speak to this? What does Jesus have to say about it?

How do you think Mary Katherine feels about her decision to pursue her craft of weaving when some people think she should be doing other things, such as helping out with the farming?

What voices does she hear that discourage her in using her gift? What kind of conflict does that create in her?

Do you think Mary Katherine is making a wise choice about how she spends the majority of her "work" time? Why or why not?

In God's eyes, you are enough as you are. Your worth is not dependent on what you can do or what you can accomplish.

Do you have trouble making decisions about how you spend your time, or do you tend to say yes to everything that comes your way out of a sense of obligation? If you are placing your sense of worth in how busy you are or what you can get done, God implores you to stop, rest, and reevaluate.

In God's eyes, you are enough as you are. Your worth is not dependent on what you can do or what you can accomplish. It's time to step away from those things that are not life-giving and to say yes to spending your time on those things with eternal value.

Talk to God

Creator God, I am tired—tired of running myself ragged and dividing my heart and energy on things that will not last. Lord, help me to know that I am NOT what I do. Though You have gifted me uniquely, help me to see that You love me regardless of my skills or strengths and that I don't have to depend on those things to give me worth and value—because they won't. I can only find that in You, Lord. Thank You for Your indescribable love. I sit at Your feet, Lord, eagerly wanting to hear from You. Amen.

As You Go

In Matthew 11:28 Jesus says, "Come to me, all you who are weary and burdened, and I will give you rest." How is God asking you to take the time to stop and rest today?

Day 5: Living Wholeheartedly

Read God's Word

"And whatever you do, whether in word or deed, do it all in the name of the Lord Jesus, giving thanks to God the Father through him."

Colossians 3:17

Reflect and Respond

In *Her Restless Heart*, Mary Katherine faces a huge decision about her future—whether or not she wants to be baptized into her Amish community. The weighty choice has been heavy on her shoulders, the pressure of such a decision paralyzing. She wonders why the decision is such a tough one to make and why the answer isn't clearer, and she finds herself constantly struggling in making the decision, even while she sleeps.

Excerpt from Chapter 13

Mary Katherine walked into her bedroom at her grandmother's house and felt the weight of the world slip from her shoulders.

She unpinned her kapp, *undressed, and hung up her clothing. After she slipped into a nightgown, she climbed into the narrow bed and felt herself melt into its softness. . . .*

Something woke her. She lay in her bed and wondered what it was, then heard it again. It sounded like the rain had the night before, pattering against the window glass. But when she turned her head, she saw that the rain was gone and the sky was blue and cloudless.

Getting out of bed, she winced as her feet hit the cold wooden floor. She went to look out the window and saw Jacob standing on the grass below. He tossed a handful of pebbles that hit the glass and then waved when he saw her.

"Come down!" he mouthed, gesturing with his hand.

She hesitated, and then she drew the curtain and flew around the room, gathering her undergarments and clothing to dress.

Mere minutes later, she ran down the stairs and joined him outside. "What are you doing here?"

"I wanted to see you. Let's go for a ride."

"Where?"

"Anywhere you want to go."

"Far away," she said, gazing past her grandmother's farm to the town that lay miles away. "I want to go far away."

When she glanced back at him, wondering why he hadn't responded, she saw that he looked sad. She didn't want him to be sad but she yearned for something . . . something she didn't know how to find. Didn't even know how to express to herself, let alone to him.

"Where are you going?"

"Hmm?" she turned and looked at him. "What?"

"Where are you going?"

Fog swirled around her, like the clouds of doubt that had surrounded her for so many months now. She stuck out her arms, trying to part it so she could see him, touch him, but it was impenetrable.

"Come back," Jacob called. "Don't go away!" His voice faded.

She'd wanted to leave but not like this, cut off from seeing him, hearing him.

But she couldn't have that—whatever it was out there—and have him, too. He was rooted here and couldn't leave. Wouldn't leave.

She woke, her cheeks wet with tears, and realized she'd been dreaming.

"You're being awfully quiet," Anna said. "What's wrong?"

Mary Katherine examined the weaving on the loom before her. She sighed. "Do you ever feel like nothing's as good when you make it as when it's in your mind, your imagination?"

Anna walked over and took a seat. She pulled her knitting needles from a nearby basket, and the familiar clacking noise began.

"Yeah. I think it's like that with anyone who does something creative. Especially artists," she said, holding up the muffler she was creating.

Laughing, Mary Katherine undid the last two rows she'd woven. "I'm not an artist."

"No? I think you are. And you're also a perfectionist."

Mary Katherine looked at her cousin. "That's the pot calling the kettle black. I've seen you unravel baby caps that look fine to me."

"Hey, they have to be as perfect as what I make for anyone else." She smiled. "Maybe even more so. They're going to be worn by someone who's considered pretty much perfect, wouldn't you say?"

"Yes, I suppose." . . .

Was it possible to achieve perfection? she wondered. Not just in creative work, but as a person? . . .

Leah walked past with the bolt of fabric to return it to its shelf. She took Anna's chair when she returned. "So what's got you looking so thoughtful?"

"If we're made in His image, why aren't we perfect?"

Her grandmother raised her brows. "Well, that's an interesting question."

"Deep for me, right?" Mary Katherine grinned.

"You've always been 'deep,'" Leah said. "Always seeking, always questioning."

"Not an easy child, right?"

Leah's smile was kind. "I'd rather have a child who's looking for answers than an easy one who just accepts everything."

Mary Katherine laughed. "Well, you got that in me, didn't you?"

"It doesn't make for an easy life though, does it, dear one? It's why you struggle so with your decision."

Sighing, Mary Katherine nodded.

Leah smoothed her hands over her skirt. Mary Katherine noted that her grandmother's hands were still beautiful, not lined or rough, even though Leah cleaned her own house and worked in her kitchen garden.

"It has occurred to me that you may be overthinking some things," Leah said slowly. "Maybe you're thinking with your head instead of your heart."

Mary Katherine rested her own hands—usually so busy—in her lap. "How can I overthink something so important? The decision is one you make for a lifetime."

"The church or marriage?"

"Well—both."

"I guess it's a matter of just what you think you'll find in the Englisch world that you've been seeking here and haven't found."

She considered that. "You mean make a list?"

Leah laughed. "You might be a creative person, but you're very practical, you know that?"

"Can someone be Amish and not be practical?" Mary Katherine teased.

"Ah, so you consider yourself Amish?" Leah returned seriously.

"I—uh . . ."

"And I would ask you what you think you'll find in a man that isn't in one you already love?"

Mary Katherine threw up her hands. "Why is it that you and Anna and Naomi seem determined to pair me with Jacob?"

Leah just smiled that wise smile of hers. "I wonder."

❖

In our quest to live the lives that God intends for us, we often come to a place where we are not sure what to do. There is a fork in the road, or a fallen tree blocks the path, or the path disappears into the woods altogether. Without any pointing arrows or "Go This Way" signs, we're left without directions about what to do. We become confused and frustrated. We overthink the solutions. We wonder, *Should it be this hard? Why isn't it clear which way I should go? Am I doing something wrong?*

Suddenly the clear, easy path turns treacherous. We start to be afraid of what we can't see, of what might be lurking out there. We wonder if God is present and why He didn't equip us better for the journey if He wanted us to walk this path. We wanted our walk to be perfect, and we're disappointed that it's not.

But none of our lives follows a path that is always clear and perfect. We face obstacles and decisions that require us to seek God and His will for our lives, and we sometimes struggle with the answers we get. We must let go of our idea of perfection and learn to trust in God's will for us. We must make the tough decisions that require us to give something up in order to get something else; we must learn that what is perfect is exactly what God has for us.

> We must let go of our idea of perfection and learn to trust in God's will for us.

Mary Katherine faces a huge, life-altering choice: whether or not to join the church. What might her life look like if she chooses to join the church? What if she chooses not to join the church? What does she give up or gain in each scenario?

Have you experienced a time when your perfect ideal of something was shattered? What happened, and how did you respond? Did it affect your view of God, and if so, how?

Though we know our lives will never be perfect, that knowledge certainly doesn't stop us from trying, does it? Whether it's getting more "stuff" or working hard to get that dream job or having some unrealistic expectations of those around us, it seems we're always thinking that the "grass is greener on the other side" and striving to get there. But when this becomes our way of living, we become broken and distracted, our hearts divided between letting God be God and taking control of our own lives again and again.

Instead, God calls us to live wholeheartedly, fully embracing where He has placed us at any given time, trusting Him to guide our decisions and leading us to the outcome He desires for us.

What do each of the following verses have to say about living whole-heartedly?

Matthew 22:37

Ephesians 6:7

Colossians 3:17

Learning to live wholeheartedly requires us to trust God and receive His love. It requires that we are committed to following God's leading and willing to step out in trust and obedience when He calls us. How is God leading you today?

Talk to God

My heart is divided, Lord. One half wants to follow You wherever You lead, and the other yearns for what I think is best for my life. Help me to have an undivided heart, to learn to listen for Your voice, and to trust Your leading. Help me to understand that the only perfect will for my life is the one You have spoken into being. I want to live for You alone, Lord. Amen.

As You Go

Colossians 3:17 says, "And whatever you do, whether in word or deed, do it all in the name of the Lord Jesus, giving thanks to God the Father through him." Are you able to say to God, "Whatever, wherever, whoever"? Ask God to give you the strength today to follow Him wherever He leads.

About the Amish

What is *rumschpringe* and what is the purpose of this practice?

Many Amish feel *rumschpringe* has been misunderstood by the *Englisch*. It is a time from the teens to the early twenties when Amish young people may experience aspects of *Englisch* life and decide whether to join the Amish church and remain a part of the community or be *Englisch*. More than 80 percent of the Amish youth choose to remain in their community and join the church. Family, faith, and community are so much a part of an Amish person's life that these connections tend to prove to be more important than anything he or she may have thought was appealing about the *Englisch* way of life.

Video Notes
A Few Minutes with Barbara

Interesting Insights:

Points I'd Like to Discuss with the Group:

Week 5
The Romantic Heart

Scripture for the Week

We love because he first loved us.

1 John 4:19 ESV

Every good and perfect gift is from above, coming down from the Father of the heavenly lights, who does not change like shifting shadows.

James 1:17

Setting the Stage

From the beginning of creation, a woman's heart was made to love; we have the capacity and desire for companionship and relationship. This week we will discover that when we are able to realize and embrace God's full, unconditional love for us, we are freed to love others fully, with an eager and open heart.

Excerpt from Chapter 16

Jamie smirked. "C'mon, everyone, grab a plate and let's eat." She carried the pizzas into the kitchen and opened them up. Breathing in the scent, she grinned. "I've heard of doghouse flowers—you know, the ones guys send after they've done something they need to apologize for. But I never heard of doghouse pizza. Guess there's a first time for everything."

Each of [the girls] took a plate piled with several slices of pizza and a can of soda into the living room. Anna won the right to choose the movie—a DVD of Tangled*—and soon Rapunzel was letting down her hair, song filled the apartment, and everyone became absorbed in the story.*

Mary Katherine was reminded of that night in the pizza place when she'd dressed in Englisch *clothes and left her hair loose—no tightly drawn bun, no pristine* kapp. *Jacob had seemed to be fascinated by her hair, staring at it.*

The fairy tale played on. The one on the television screen, that is. She wasn't so sheltered in her community that she didn't know about fairy tales. She'd read a number of them in books that she'd checked out from the library bookmobile. Maybe she'd even had a few girlish dreams of a handsome man falling in love with her.

But in the end, she was too practical to really believe in them. She didn't understand the Englisch *fascination with such. Wasn't it better to look at love the way the Plain people did? You didn't wait for some handsome stranger—you dated the boy you'd grown up seeing in church, in* schul, *at singings and other social events. You knew you'd be his partner in his life's work—and he in yours if you chose to work as well as raise your* kinner—*so you made certain that your love ran true and deep and it wasn't just some story you'd made up about him.*

Just how true and deep had Jacob's love been for her? she asked herself. If you loved the way you should, you didn't jump to conclusions about the other person. Did you?

Jamie got up from the sofa to get more pizza. "Something wrong with yours? I got pepperoni, your favorite," she whispered.

"I'm not very hungry," she confessed.

"Come on, let's go into the kitchen and talk."

"Ssh," Anna hissed, her attention on the television set.

Mary Katherine got up and followed Jamie into the kitchen. "I really don't want to talk anymore. It just hurts too much."

Jamie gestured at a chair and took a seat. "I want to try out something I learned in Psych class this semester. Psychology class," she explained.

She narrowed her eyes. "You don't cut up animals in that class, do you?"

Jamie laughed. "No, that's biology and we do it on the computer. No animals are harmed in biology class at the college—actually, in a lot of those classes in other colleges and high schools."

She took a deep breath. "Okay, let's do this little experiment. When's the last time you felt this bad? Who hurt you?"

"You know the answer to that," Mary Katherine said. "My father."

"So you're feeling like you did something wrong when you didn't?"

Mary Katherine nodded, not sure why Jamie was asking such questions.

"You said once you didn't want to date because you weren't sure if you were going to join the church. But do you think maybe you were afraid of being hurt by a guy? I mean, if you didn't feel loved by your own father . . ."

She was right, of course. Although she'd really said as much to Jamie, Mary Katherine knew it was true for her, too. Sighing, she nodded.

"Do you think you overreacted?"

Mary Katherine stared at her. "You're not saying I shouldn't be upset with Jacob?"

"No, no, of course not. I'd tell him to his face he was a jerk. Anyone who sees the two of you together can see that you love him." She patted Mary Katherine's hand. "And anyone can see that the man is head over heels in love with you. I think he's a little insecure and maybe jumped to conclusions, reacted to that nosy woman."

"What's he got to be insecure about?"

"I don't know. But from what you told me, it sounds like he is. I think you should ask him about it." She grinned. "Maybe not until you cool down. But you owe it to yourself to find out and then see if the two of you can work it out."

"You're right. And you're right about another thing. Remember you said I really didn't want to leave the community, because I was Amish? Well, I'm going to take instruction to join the church."

Jamie didn't even blink. "I knew it!" She clasped Mary Katherine's hands and squeezed them. "It feels like a good decision?"

"It feels like a good decision."

She glanced at the pizza box. "I want another slice of pizza, but I guess that would make me a little piggy, wouldn't it."

"Ya, a little oinkette," Mary Katherine agreed with a straight face.

Jamie stared at her and then she laughed. "So, the little Amish girl is starting to get her sense of humor back. That's a good sign."

"I'm not little, but I'm an Amish girl," she said, grinning. "We'll see how it goes with the Amish boy when I talk to him. I don't intend to be a pushover just because I love the man."

"You go, girl!"

Anna came into the kitchen. "Have you guys eaten all the pizza?"

"Not even close. And there's ice cream in the freezer. I think we should celebrate, don't you?"

"Celebrate what?" Naomi asked as she put her empty plate in the sink.

"Mary Katherine taking classes to join the church."

"Oh, I always knew she'd do it," Anna said airily.

"Oh you did, did you?"

"Of course. What kind of ice cream?"

Jamie winked at Mary Katherine as she got up to look in the freezer. "There's Rocky Road and butter pecan."

"Rocky Road," said Anna.

"Butter pecan," said Naomi.

"Mary Katherine?"

She grinned at Jamie and her cousins. "I think I'd rather have butter pecan than Rocky Road."

[Mary Katherine said,] "I'm going to take instruction to join the church." Jamie didn't even blink. "I knew it!"

127

Jamie hugged her and handed her the carton of ice cream. "Smooth roads ahead, huh?"

"Ya," Mary Katherine said fervently. "Please, God, smooth roads ahead."

Day 1: Fairy Tale Expectations

Read God's Word

". . . I have loved you with an everlasting love."

Jeremiah 31:3

Reflect and Respond

The fairy tale always begins with a girl. Sometimes she's drop-dead gorgeous; sometimes she's girl-next-door cute and quirky. Sometimes she's looking for a guy; other times she's looking for something else and the guy gets in the way. But in every case, the basic premise of every tale and modern-day chick flick is the same: against many odds and through many twists and turns, entwined with a huge dose of luck and dogged determination, the girl gets her guy, and they are impossibly, irrefutably, irresistibly happy. You know the ending: *And they lived happily ever after.* But have you ever wondered what comes next in the story?

A recent online cartoon depicts various Disney princesses as desperate housewives, sitting together complaining about their men. Belle (from *Beauty and the Beast*) says that her husband is such an animal. Cinderella laments that her husband still drives a pumpkin. Snow White complains that she's constantly left alone with seven little ones. As they say, the fairy tale is over for these princesses.

Why do you think we women tend to love a good fairy tale?

In *Her Restless Heart*, Mary Katherine realizes that she doesn't put much stock in fairy tales. Reread the following excerpt included in the introduction to Week 5.

Excerpt from Chapter 16

The fairy tale played on. The one on the television screen, that is. [Mary Katherine] wasn't so sheltered in her community that she didn't know about fairy tales. She'd read a number of them in books that she'd checked out from the library bookmobile. Maybe she'd even had a few girlish dreams of a handsome man falling in love with her.

But in the end, she was too practical to really believe in them. She didn't understand the Englisch *fascination with such. Wasn't it better to look at love the way the Plain people did? You didn't wait for some handsome stranger—you dated the boy you'd grown up seeing in church, in* schul, *at singings and other social events. You knew you'd be his partner in his life's work—and he in yours if you chose to work as well as raise your* kinner—*so you made certain that your love ran true and deep and it wasn't just some story you'd made up about him.*

Have you ever had your own fairy-tale experience? What happened and how did it make you feel? How long did that feeling last?

How do you feel about the practical Amish view of love relationships? Do you lean more toward the practical side of love or the romantic side, or are you somewhere in the middle?

When we hope for the perfect fairy tale, what expectations does that put on our relationships and marriages? How do you think those expectations affect our relationships?

We all long to experience the adventure, elation, and resolution of the fairy tale, and we're often disappointed when life doesn't measure up.

We all long to experience the adventure, elation, and resolution of the fairy tale, and we're often disappointed when life doesn't measure up. So how do we cope when everyday life throws cold water on the fire of our relationships? When

who we thought was Mr. Right doesn't call after the second date? When the unbridled romance we were expecting is something more like lukewarm companionship? When our deep desire to love and be loved is harder than we expected? We turn our eyes toward the One who loves us beyond what we could ever hope for.

In Jeremiah 31:3, the Lord says, "I have loved you with an everlasting love." In his letter to the Ephesians, Paul prays that his fellow Christians will "have power, together with all the Lord's holy people, to grasp how wide and long and high and deep is the love of Christ, and to know this love that surpasses knowledge—that you may be filled to the measure of all the fullness of God" (3:18-19). Talk about a dramatic kind of love!

Have you ever considered that you are already in a grand love story, written before the beginning of time? In this love story, a white knight—a Savior—has come and rescued you so that you might have the love that you've always dreamed of. He calls you Beloved, and He gave up everything so that you could stand at His side.

In Christ, we have the ultimate "fairy tale," and no other relationship on Earth can replace the perfect one that He offers. Ephesians 2:4-5 says, "But God, being rich in mercy, because of the great love with which he loved us, even when we were dead in our trespasses, made us alive together with Christ—by grace you have been saved" (ESV).

How does knowing that you are completely and unconditionally loved by God free you to experience healthy love relationships with others?

> Have you ever considered that you are already in a grand love story, written before the beginning of time?

Talk to God

God, You are love, and I pray that You will help me grasp how wide and long and high and deep Your love is for me. I know that You are the ultimate love of my life and that You will never fail me or leave me. Resting in that love, I know that I can love others with all my heart and devote myself to them with the love that You flow through me. I love you, Lord. Thank You for loving me. Amen.

As You Go

Today, ask God to reveal to you the fairy-tale expectations that you are placing on your relationships, and ask Him to lead you as you strive to show love to others and accept love from them.

Day 2: Looking for Love

Read God's Word

*At the time G*OD *made Earth and Heaven, before any grasses or shrubs had sprouted from the ground—G*OD *hadn't yet sent rain on Earth, nor was there anyone around to work the ground (the whole Earth was watered by underground springs)—G*OD *formed Man out of dirt from the ground and blew into his nostrils the breath of life. The Man came alive—a living soul!*

*Then G*OD *planted a garden in Eden, in the east. He put the Man he had just made in it. . . .*

*G*OD *said, "It's not good for the Man to be alone; I'll make him a helper, a companion." So G*OD *formed from the dirt of the ground all the animals of the field and all the birds of the air. He brought them to the Man to see what he would name them. Whatever the Man called each living creature, that was its name. The Man named the cattle, named the birds of the air, named the wild animals; but he didn't find a suitable companion.*

*G*OD *put the Man into a deep sleep. As he slept he removed one of his ribs and replaced it with flesh. G*OD *then used the rib that he had taken from the Man to make Woman and presented her to the Man.*

The Man said, "Finally! Bone of my bone, flesh of my flesh! Name her Woman for she was made from Man."

Therefore a man leaves his father and mother and embraces his wife. They become one flesh.

Genesis 2:5-9a, 18-25a *THE MESSAGE*

Reflect and Respond

From the very beginning, we women were created for companionship. We were made with a great capacity to love and a great desire to be loved in return. Whether married or single, we all have this need for love and companionship. And though God *is* and should be our number-one source for fulfillment, the desire to walk through life together with another is a God-given desire that was meant for our good. After God created Adam, He said, "It's not good for the Man to be alone" (Genesis 2:18 *THE MESSAGE*). He wanted Adam to have someone to share his life with, someone whom he could hold and talk to and laugh with. Adam needed Eve, and she needed him.

Even though the desire for intimate companionship—the desire to walk through life with another—is given to us by God, have you ever struggled with this desire, feeling that it is somehow less than spiritual? Why or why not?

Marriage didn't just happen; God created it. After Eve was created, Adam said, "'This is now bone of my bones and flesh of my flesh.' . . . That is why a man leaves his father and mother and is united to his wife, and they become one flesh" (Genesis 2:23-24). God conceived of and ordained marriage, and therefore it is good.

Why do you think God created marriage?

In order for a marriage relationship to thrive, it must be put into proper perspective as secondary to your relationship with God.

Based on your own life experiences, what is your view of marriage? Do you see it as a good thing, something to desire and celebrate, or do you have a doubting or cynical view of marriage? Explain your response.

What has been your approach to romantic love in life—all-in, head-over-heels, or slower and more cautious? Why do you think that is?

Apart from our relationship with God, marriage is most likely the deepest and most intimate relationship we can experience here on Earth. It is a wonderful thing to be able to walk through life's ups and downs with another person, although fallible, and to experience the love of God through someone else's love and care. But in order for a marriage relationship to thrive, it must be put into proper perspective as secondary to your relationship with God.

In addition to having the proper perspective, a thriving marriage also requires hard work. Relationships are hard. And in order to be able to love someone else well, we first need to know and be filled with the love of God. First John 4:19 says, "We love because he first loved us" (ESV). God wants us to learn to love each other well.

Leah tells Mary Katherine that there was a reason we weren't put on Earth by ourselves: we're supposed to learn something from other people, and they from us. What is something you think God wants us to learn from one another through marriage?

Do you think Mary Katherine views marriage as a good thing? Why or why not?

Do you struggle with keeping your marriage—or significant relationships—in proper perspective to your relationship with God? If so, in what ways?

Talk to God

Lord, You have given us the desire to love and connect with others. Help me to know that this desire for relationship with others is good and that You encourage it while remembering that You want me to desire You above all else. Thank You for Your love and care for me. Amen.

As You Go

How is God speaking to you today about your desire for love and companionship? Are you looking to Him first to meet that need, or are you trying to find it in other relationships?

Day 3: The Miracle of Love

Read God's Word

Every good and perfect gift is from above, coming down from the Father of the heavenly lights, who does not change like shifting shadows.

James 1:17

Reflect and Respond

We all walk through life bearing the marks of our pasts, and the ways in which we approach our love relationships are certainly affected by our past experiences and hurts. In the novel, Mary Katherine becomes very upset when Jacob accuses her of seeing another man, Daniel, behind his back. Mary Katherine is confused and upset by his accusations; she is hurt that he would think such things about her. In her pain, she is reminded of how her father has hurt her in the past, and she finds it hard to forgive Jacob, wondering if he, like her father, will continue to break her faith and trust.

Excerpt from Chapter 17

Leah glanced over at Mary Katherine. "You're being awfully quiet."

Mary Katherine poked her finger at the last few rows she'd woven. "Something's wrong with this."

Anna rose and came to stand behind her. "Looks fine to me."

She shook her head. "There, don't you see the flaw?"

"Nee. Naomi, you come look."

Naomi tucked her needle safely in her quilt, stood up, and walked over to study the pattern. "I don't see anything, either. Sorry, Mary Katherine." She walked over and resumed her seat. . . .

[Mary Katherine] pulled out a row, then another and another, until she'd pulled out a half-foot and her breath was coming hard. Tears burned behind her eyelids.

"Kumm," her grandmother urged, taking her by her shoulders and helping her rise. "Let's go into the back room and talk."

She jerked her head up and found Anna and Naomi regarding her with sympathy.

"Lock the door and turn the sign to 'Closed,'" Leah told Anna.

"No, no, if a customer comes out in the rain I don't want her to go away disappointed."

"We haven't had a customer in two hours," Leah said. "I don't think we have to worry about that."

"I'll watch the shop," Anna volunteered. "If we get a herd of customers, I'll yell for you."

So Mary Katherine followed Leah and Naomi into the back room and watched as Naomi made tea. She rubbed her forehead. It always seemed to be hurting lately. Crying herself to sleep some nights probably didn't help. Lying awake others didn't either.

"I remember telling you once that a cup of tea didn't cure everything," [Mary Katherine] said, looking at her grandmother. "You said that it's the talking that does that."

Leah nodded. "And it's time you did some talking. To Jacob. You've avoided him long enough. You hurt. Tell him so. Either the two of you will fix it or you'll walk away from each other. Pray, talk, and then know it's in God's hands."

Such simple words. Such a huge task. She didn't think she was up to it. "I'm afraid," she whispered.

Her grandmother reached for her hands and held them. "Ach, I know. But it's not fair to blame Jacob for too much hurt, isn't it?"

"But he was the one who hurt me."

Leah shook her head. "You've been carrying around a lot of hurt for a long time."

"My father."

Nodding, Leah patted her hand. "It's made you afraid to love. Afraid to trust."

"You have to give him another chance," Naomi said quietly. "He's tried to say he's sorry."

"And that's supposed to be enough?" Mary Katherine asked. "What if he just keeps hurting me and expecting another chance?"

"You won't know until you give him a second chance," Naomi told her. "Then you can decide if you go forward . . ." She paused. "Or not."

How have your past experiences shaped the way you've approached your love relationships?

How does Mary Katherine's relationship with Jacob compare to her relationship with her father?

What do you think Mary Katherine needs to do to move past the hurt of her past and embrace a future with Jacob?

God is our Healer, and He is able to lift the hurt and pain of our pasts from our shoulders and bear it on His own. He gives us new life and hope and allows us to start fresh, supported by His great love for us.

In Psalm 103:1-5, David sings,

> *Praise the Lord, my soul; all my inmost being, praise his holy name.*
> *Praise the Lord, my soul, and forget not all his benefits—*
> *who forgives all your sins and heals all your diseases,*
> *who redeems your life from the pit and crowns you with love and compassion,*
> *who satisfies your desires with good things so that your youth is renewed like the eagle's.*

We must turn over our past hurts to God and allow Him to heal us and quiet our fears so that we can confidently move forward in the relationships He has given us.

When it comes to our relationships, we must turn over our past hurts to God and allow Him to heal us and quiet our fears so that we can confidently move forward in the relationships He has given us. We must trust that God is the One Who heals our hearts so that we are free to love others fully—without fear.

Read James 1:17. What does this verse say about God's nature, and what assurance does that give you?

Mary Katherine's mother, Miriam, has had to put up with a surly husband for many years, but she still hasn't given up hope that God can redeem and restore their relationship. She understands that she and Isaac haven't always been the best example of marriage for Mary Katherine, but she encourages her daughter not to shut the door on love.

Excerpt from Chapter 12

Her mother rocked and stared off into the distance. "You were right to stand up for yourself today [with your father]." Glancing at Mary Katherine, she . . . sighed. "I know that you young women think some of us older wives are—what's the term?"

"Doormats?"

Miriam winced. "Yes. Doormats. In trying to do as the Bible says and submit to our husbands, well, sometimes maybe we lean too much into our own understanding, ya?"

Mary Katherine thought about Miriam's words, remembering how the Bible said not to lean into your own understanding . . .

"Well, it's done, and maybe your father will think on what we've both said. I'm hoping that he knows that if we didn't love him we wouldn't try to help him understand he can be a better man if he changes a little."

"I don't know," Mary Katherine said. She gestured at the table between them. "I'm afraid I think Dat's like that table. He can't change."

"Well, I believe in miracles," Miriam said, looking more serene than Mary Katherine had ever seen her. "If I didn't, I might not have stayed with your father all these years in spite of what the Ordnung says about marriage and divorce."

She smiled as she watched the wind ruffle the purple spears of the hyacinths Jacob had planted a few feet from where they were sitting on the porch. "Maybe you need to believe in the miracle of love yourself, ya?"

What do you think Miriam means by "the miracle of love"?

How is God asking you to believe in that miracle—that gift—today?

Talk to God

Heavenly Father, I praise You that You do not change like shifting shadows. I can trust that You are Who You say You are and that You will do what You say You will do. Take my past hurts and all my pain and transform it, Lord, allowing me

to let go of my fears and receive Your goodness and love so that I can love others fully and freely. Amen.

As You Go

Proverbs 3:5-6 says, "Trust GOD from the bottom of your heart; don't try to figure out everything on your own. Listen for GOD's voice in everything you do, everywhere you go; he's the one who will keep you on track" (*THE MESSAGE*). How have you been leaning on your own understanding when it comes to your relationships? Today, remember that God wants you to rely on Him instead.

Day 4: Love and Respect

Read God's Word

Submit to one another out of reverence for Christ. Wives, submit your-selves to your own husbands as you do to the Lord. For the husband is the head of the wife as Christ is the head of the church, his body, of which he is the Savior. Now as the church submits to Christ, so also wives should submit to their husbands in everything.

Husbands, love your wives, just as Christ loved the church and gave himself up for her to make her holy, cleansing her by the washing with water through the word, and to present her to himself as a radiant church, without stain or wrinkle or any other blemish, but holy and blameless. In this same way, husbands ought to love their wives as their own bodies. He who loves his wife loves himself. After all, no one ever hated their own body, but they feed and care for their body, just as Christ does the church—for we are members of his body. "For this reason a man will leave his father and mother and be united to his wife, and the two will become one flesh." This is a profound mystery—but I am talking about Christ and the church. However, each one of you also must love his wife as he loves himself, and the wife must respect her husband.

Ephesians 5:21-33

Reflect and Respond

Our culture sends us all kinds of mixed messages about what an ideal dating relationship and an ideal marriage should look like, including the roles of husbands and wives. In the world's perspective, the good of the individual is often valued above the partnership, encouraging a battle of the sexes that rarely finds a favorable conclusion.

Too often it feels that women today are caught in the middle of this battle, struggling to understand what it means to have a good marriage. There is a lot of confusion and emotion surrounding the roles of husbands and wives, and more and more marriages are suffering because of it. Women want to be good wives to their husbands and to be valued and fulfilled as women. But they don't always know how to make both happen.

What would you say are the messages and/or expectations in our culture today regarding the roles of husbands and wives and what it takes to make a marriage good?

Women want to be good wives to their husbands and to be valued and fulfilled as women. But they don't always know how to make both happen.

Based on what you know about the Amish, what are their traditional beliefs about marriage and the roles of husband and wife? (If you are reading the novel, which characters give us insight into these beliefs— and how?)

There are (and always will be) countless perspectives vying for a voice on this issue, but we should be concerned with only one: God's. What does God say about marriage and the roles of husbands and wives?

Reread Ephesians 5:21-33. What is your initial response or reaction to this oft-quoted passage in Ephesians? What emotions does it stir in you?

Two key words in this passage are *love* and *respect*. Although throughout the ages many people have used the "wives submit to your husbands" command to demean and subdue, it is clear that this is *not* what God intends in these verses! God does not intend for women to be lesser partners or to be treated in a demeaning or dismissive way. As a matter of fact, husbands are instructed to love—cherish—their wives as Christ loved the church. And how did Christ do that? He gave up everything—His own safety, comfort, and even His life—in order to restore the church (His bride) to the full, rich life that was meant for her.

It's also important to note that these verses do not support abuse of any kind—verbal, emotional, or physical. Abuse is never acceptable in God's sight and certainly is not condoned by any Scripture in the Bible.

Paul begins this important passage in Ephesians by saying, "Submit to one another out of reverence for Christ" (v. 21). Why do you think he specifies that we should submit to one another "out of reverence for Christ"?

What are some examples of what it means for both husbands and wives to submit to one another?

What do the following verses have to say about how we should treat one another?

1 Corinthians 13:4-7

Galatians 5:22-23

Reread Ephesians 5:33. What do you think it means for a wife to respect her husband? What might this look like?

What are some ways a husband can love his wife as Christ loved the church?

If you are reading the novel, how does Jacob demonstrate for Mary Katherine that he has a correct biblical view of what a husband should be?

Talk to God

Loving God, I desire to know and understand—and (if married) to follow—the guidelines for marriage that You have given in Your Word. Open my spiritual ears so that I can hear Your voice above all the voices that seek to confuse and mislead me in this area. Teach me what true respect looks like in marriage, and help me to love as You love, Lord. Amen.

As You Go

This topic can be very emotionally charged for us women. Ask God to help you put your emotions aside so that you can listen to His words and hear His voice, which is full of love and gentleness. How is He speaking to you today?

Day 5: Appreciating Differences

Read God's Word

"A new commandment I give to you, that you love one another; as I have loved you, that you also love one another. By this all will know that you are My disciples, if you have love for one another."
John 13:34-35 NKJV

Reflect and Respond

While marriage is a sacred union of two souls, it also is the union of two separate people, each with unique personalities, preferences, and perspectives. Sometimes those differences between two partners are small and insignificant; other times the differences seem vast and disparate. Often these differences can cause arguments between husband and wife, yet they also can make the union stronger and richer than ever thought possible.

Like much of the Amish community, Mary Katherine's family were farmers, and being the only child, she was required to work on the farm alongside her mother and father. She disliked the tasks he had to do on the farm and resented her father's penchant for assigning her the most distasteful chores. As a result, she came to hate farming and was all too happy to escape to the safety of her grandmother's shop.

But Jacob loves farming, and he hopes that one day Mary Katherine will come to love and appreciate it as much as he does.

Excerpt from Chapter 13

It was Jacob's favorite season.

He knew many farmers preferred late summer or fall, when they reaped what they'd sowed, when they harvested the crops they'd toiled over for so long.

But there was something about spring that made it his favorite. A whole world of possibilities stretched out in front of him. . . . He could change everything out—rotate his crops. Plant seed for new varieties. The weather was never certain, but he never shrank from a challenge—not with God on his side.

For the longer he farmed, the more he came to depend on Him and acknowledge His will and His wisdom in his life.

He walked his fields and every so often found himself glancing out at the road, wishing that Mary Katherine would visit as she had that day after she'd taught that class. Now that her mother was better and she'd moved back in with her grandmother, he hoped he'd see her happy again.

There was nothing better than Mary Katherine happy.

He couldn't figure out any excuse to go by her shop, and besides, it was coming up on a busy time for him again. Sighing when the only vehicle that passed was an Englischer's car, he went back to walking the fields.

Memories of working these fields often came to him as he walked them to check on the progress of the crop, to see what he needed to do to nurture it.

Amish children learned early how to farm, and most of them loved it. He frowned when he thought about how Mary Katherine didn't feel that way about it.

It was easy to understand her dislike of farm work. Her father wasn't an easy man and seldom cracked a smile. Jacob figured that Mary Katherine, with her gentle nature and her artistic bent, had had a hard time of it being around such a critical man. Then, too, Isaac hadn't had a big, sturdy son to help him with the harder farm chores, only a rather delicate young daughter.

And Isaac considered it a waste of money to hire outside help.

Farm work was hard, no doubt, and not for the weak or squeamish or lazy. Definitely not for those who hated it. But he wasn't sure Mary Katherine hated it.

He was still hoping that she didn't really hate it, that she'd developed an . . . aversion to it because of her father.

And optimist that he was, he hoped he could work on that.

A glance at the position of the sun told him the approximate time. Clear skies and low humidity meant he and Ben would begin planting the seed the next day.

If he hadn't had his head bent, watching where he was walking, he might have missed the little clutch of violets pushing up from the earth.

He heard a car door slam and looked up to see Mary Katherine emerging from a car he recognized as one from Nick Brannigan's taxi business. A rush of pleasure shot through him. Acting on instinct, he plucked up the flowers and carried them with him. It was hard to keep his stride steady and not hurry too much.

"Gut-n-owed," *she called as she picked her way through one of the rows.*

"Stay there, don't get your shoes dirty!" *he called.*

The setting sun outlined her slender figure; the wind fluttered the skirts of her dress and the ties of her bonnet.

She smiled when he approached and held out the flowers.

"I found these just as I heard the car."

"They must be the first violets of the season. And white ones. You don't often find them." *She raised them to her nose and inhaled.* "Mmm, they smell so sweet. Danki."

"My mamm *used to have the most beautiful garden out in front of the house."*

They walked together to the front porch, and he gestured for her to have a seat.

"I helped her take the flowers and bushes to her new home when she remarried," *he told her.* "I knew I wouldn't have the time to keep it up. Maybe not even the knowledge to do so."

"You're a farmer. You couldn't make her garden grow?"

"I'm a crop farmer, not a flower grower," *he said.* "And she needed the things she'd nurtured. They were like her kinner *to her."*

"I had a little garden at my parents years ago. Dat *didn't give me much time to work in it. Said it was more important to raise vegetables we could eat."*

"My mamm *always says a woman's soul needs flowers."*

143

In order for a husband and wife to have a relationship that is rich and vibrant, each must learn to embrace what the other loves. They must celebrate each other's strengths and learn how those strengths can complement the strengths of the other, making the relationship stronger.

If you are married, how alike are you and your spouse? What are your differences?

If you are not married, how alike and different are or were your parents?

Each spouse's strengths matter, and learning to love and appreciate those gifts and how they complement the other's gifts makes a relationship strong.

Have those differences been a struggle in your marriage—or your parents' marriage? If so, how? How are you learning—or how did your parents learn—to embrace those differences to make a stronger marriage?

As we discussed in Week 3, God has made each of us with intention and love, giving each of us specific gifts and strengths that make us unique. Each spouse's strengths matter, and learning to love and appreciate those gifts and how they complement the other's gifts makes a relationship strong.

Read the following passages. Circle phrases or words that speak to you.

For as we have many members in one body, but all the members do not have the same function, so we, being many, are one body in Christ, and individually members of one another. Having then gifts differing according to the grace that is given to us, let us use them.
Romans 12:4-6 NKJV

For as the body is one and has many members, but all the members of that one body, being many, are one body, so also is Christ. . . . For in

144

fact the body is not one member but many. . . . If the whole body were an eye, where would be the hearing? If the whole were hearing, where would be the smelling? But now God has set the members, each one of them, in the body just as He pleased. And if they were all one member, where would the body be? But now indeed there are many members, yet one body.

1 Corinthians 12:12, 14, 17-20 NKJV

"A new commandment I give to you, that you love one another; as I have loved you, that you also love one another. By this all will know that you are My disciples, if you have love for one another."

John 13:34-35 NKJV

When we are able to rest in the gifts God has given us, knowing that God created each of us uniquely and that we have a role to fill in the world, we can accept the gifts of others in our lives. We don't have to compete or one-up each other, quarrelling about whose gift is better or more useful; instead, we can celebrate, embrace, and appreciate the richness that others bring into our lives.

Jacob loves Mary Katherine for who she is, and once Mary Katherine learns to love Jacob for who he is, she recognizes the amazing man that God has made him to be. Only then is she able to rest in the assurance of his love for her and the hope of a bright future together.

Excerpt from Chapter 17

[Jacob took Mary Katherine] to a small park that bordered a pond. After a long, cold winter, it was a pleasure to spread out a quilt and sit on it. The sun felt warm on her face. Daffodils danced as a gentle breeze drifted through them.

Mary Katherine smiled as she watched a mother duck lead her little ducklings to the water.

Jacob reached over and ran a fingertip across her lips, his eyes dark with desire. "I've missed that smile. I've missed you."

"Me, too." His touch was sending shivers through her. Her cheeks heated, and she found her breath started coming faster.

His hand moved to cup her cheek and he moved closer, bending to kiss her.

An Englisch couple walked past and looked at them curiously.

"We could go someplace where we can be more private."

"Is that a good idea?" she asked, licking her suddenly dry lips.

> When we are able to rest in the gifts God has given us, knowing that God created each of us uniquely and that we have a role to fill in the world, we can accept the gifts of others in our lives.

"No. You're right."

"I don't want to be right." Disappointed, she opened the top lid of the picnic basket, then shut it again.

He sighed heavily. "I just planted my fields."

She crossed her arms over her chest. "Well, I'm sorry, but I don't really care about that right now." She could hear the slight note of petulance in her voice, but she didn't care.

"You hate farming that much?"

"No," she said at last. *"I'll love it because I love you."*

Imagine what might happen in Mary Katherine and Jacob's relationship once they marry. What do you think their relationship and life together will look like?

Talk to God

If married. . .

Lord, I know (all too well) that You have made my husband and me in different, unique ways. Rather than fight those differences, I pray that You would help me appreciate them. Help the two of us work together so that our strengths and weaknesses complement one another, making our relationship richer and brighter because of it. Thank You for the man you have made him to be. Help me to encourage him and nurture his strengths and gifts so that he learns to serve You with all his heart. Amen.

If single. . .

Lord, I know (all too well) that You have made each of us different and unique. Rather than fight those differences, I pray that You would help me to appreciate them. Help me to work together with the important people in my life so that our strengths and weaknesses complement one another, making our relationships richer and brighter. Thank You for each and every one—and for the unique individuals you have made them to be. Help me to encourage them and nurture their strengths and gifts so that they may grow to serve You with all their hearts. Amen.

As You Go

In learning to appreciate our differences, sometimes we need to learn to speak words of affirmation and love to the people we love. How is God leading you to speak words of love and encouragement to someone today?

About the Amish

What are some of the practices related to dating in the Amish community?

We've all heard the expression "I was the last to know." Sometimes Amish parents don't know that their son or daughter is engaged—or to whom—until the engagement is announced.

Why the secrecy? An Amish man or woman values privacy and does not want everyone to know the intimate details of his or her life. In a small community where everyone does everything together—church in each other's homes, close working relationships, a small geographic area—it would be very disruptive for others to know who they are interested in pursuing romantically.

Couples "date" by attending singings that the parents host. At these singings, young people get together to share food and an evening of singing hymns. Some couples will go for buggy rides, but who is with whom is not discussed. Even after the parents know about an engagement, the information may be closely guarded until the announcement is made in church shortly before the wedding.

In the Lancaster County area of Pennsylvania, the family of a young woman who is engaged will sometimes hide a crop of celery among other crops for the upcoming wedding. Why celery? The vegetable is featured on the wedding day table. It is used in creamed celery, in the chicken stuffing entrée, and even in glass vases for snacking and decoration.

There are other customs that seem different to us but make sense to the Amish. For example, they choose to follow traditional roles that work for them, including sitting with their own sex in church services. Those in the *Englisch* community who have attended same-sex schools or colleges may better understand this separation, acknowledging that it is easier to concentrate fully when undistracted by the opposite sex.

It is good to remember that different is different—not strange or bad. Although secrecy or privacy about dating might not work for us in the *Englisch* community, it works well for the Amish, who live in small communities where families remain for generations and everyone knows everyone else. Perhaps the reason why Amish marriages last so long is because couples know each other for years and years before they get married.

Video Notes
A Few Minutes with Barbara

Interesting Insights:

Points I'd Like to Discuss with the Group:

Week 6
The Satisfied Heart

Scripture for the Week

O God, you are my God,
earnestly I seek you;
my soul thirsts for you,
my body longs for you,
in a dry and weary land
where there is no water.
I have seen you in the sanctuary
and beheld your power and your glory.
Because your love is better than life,
my lips will glorify you.
I will praise you as long as I live,
and in your name I will lift up my hands.
My soul will be satisfied as with the richest of foods;
with singing lips my mouth will praise you.

Psalm 63:1-5

Setting the Stage

Though the paths that our lives take often lead us through ups and downs, joys and sorrows, the Lord is continually renewing us and drawing us closer to Him. This week we will learn how putting our hope, trust, and faith in God allows us to live fully and freely, enabling us to take each step as it comes, confident in His love for us and in the assurance that He will never leave or forsake us. This hope gives us a boldness to step out in faith and follow where God leads—our hearts fully satisfied in Him.

Excerpt from Chapter 14

Another church service, and God hadn't talked to her.
Mary Katherine sighed as she watched the women sitting around her get up and leave the room.

She supposed it was ridiculous to expect God to talk to her while others were—while the lay ministers talked and everyone sang and attention was generally on other things.

Maybe He just wasn't interested in communicating with her when she hadn't talked to him much in a long time. But she'd had a good reason. He hadn't listened to her when she'd been so unhappy on her parents' farm. She'd prayed and prayed and prayed, and the only reason she was out of there was because her grandmother had come to ask her parents if she could live with her and help her there and at the shop. . . .

"You're looking thoughtful."

Mary Katherine looked up and saw Jenny Bontrager smiling down at her. "I . . . guess."

"May I?" Jenny gestured at the chair beside her.

Nodding, she watched the other woman take a seat.

"I should help with the food, but I thought I'd say hello. I wanted to tell you that the pillows I bought from you are really pretty in my living room. I thought I'd order another set in blue for my friend, Joy."

"I'm so glad you like them. And thanks for the order." . . . Mary Katherine withdrew a notebook from her purse and jotted a note to herself about the order. . . . She hesitated, then took a deep breath. "Can I ask you something?"

"Sure."

Before Mary Katherine could frame the question, Matthew, Jenny's husband, appeared in the doorway. She held up two fingers in some kind of signal he understood, and he left them.

"I'm sorry, this isn't a good time for you."

Jenny smiled. "It's a fine time. What's your question?"

"How did you make your decision to become Amish? I mean, you'd been Englisch *all your life."*

"I always felt very comfortable here." Jenny brushed at imaginary lint on the skirt of her dress. "My father grew up here, and though he chose not to become Amish and stay in the community, he let me come here during the summers to visit my grandmother."

Several men came in and began moving the chairs around for the snack that would be served.

"Let's go out onto the porch, shall we?"

Mary Katherine followed her there, and they stood out of the way of people coming and going.

"I fell in love with Matthew, the boy next door, so to speak, but I went away to college. Then I went overseas, was injured, and ended up back here."

She stared off at the fields, and Mary Katherine wondered what she was thinking.

"I came back to Paradise feeling like God had abandoned me. But then after a while it seemed like everything became clearer. While I was recuperating, it seemed like everything clicked."

"Especially with a certain man," Mary Katherine teased.

"Yes," Jenny said with a reminiscent smile. "But it's not an easy decision to change your faith to marry. Especially to this faith."

She glanced down at her Plain dress, then looked up as a buggy passed. "It was still a bit of a culture shock, even though I knew more about it than most Englisch."

She looked at Mary Katherine. "Joining the church is a big decision. It can't be done quickly or lightly. I think most everyone understands that. Don't let the bishop or anyone else make you feel you have to do it by a certain time if you're not comfortable. . . . Anything else you want to ask me?"

Mary Katherine shook her head. "No. Thanks."

Jenny touched her hand. "No, thank you."

"Me? For what?"

"For reminding me of all I have to be grateful for now."

Mary Katherine jumped when she heard a squeal from the other end of the porch.

She looked up and saw a little boy who was the image of Matthew toddling toward them with outstretched arms.

"There he is!" Jenny exclaimed, chuckling. "Mr. Mischief!" She turned to Mary Katherine. "He kept us up with teething pain last night and then was out of his crib this morning playing with the cat."

Mary Katherine sat there for a long time after Jenny left, thinking about what she'd said. . . .

"I think someone's looking for you," her grandmother told her as she entered the kitchen. . . .

[Mary Katherine] found her mother laughing and talking with her next-door neighbor.

"We came in late, so we sat in the back," her mother said. "I saw you talking to Jenny. Such a nice woman." She glanced at the plate in Mary Katherine's hand. "That looks good. Lizzie, we should get something to eat."

"This is for you." She handed her the plate and kissed her on her cheek. "What would you like to drink?"

"That iced tea looks good," she said, jerking her head toward the woman at the next table who was drinking it. "Are you going to join us?"

"Sure. Let me go get your tea and some food for myself."

Her mind [elsewhere], she didn't see someone in front of her until she ran into him.

"Oh, sorry!"

"No problem," Jacob said, grinning. "I was just looking for you."

"I'm getting my mother something to drink," she told him.

His eyebrows went up. "She's here? I'll go say hello. Then maybe we can talk?" He turned, then glanced over his shoulder, and there was that look on his face—that look he'd been giving her—before he strode away. . . .

She found it hard to have a conversation with her mother when one person after another had to welcome [Miriam] back after her [health scare and] absence, but it did Mary Katherine's heart good to see that her mother had been missed. Through the years, Miriam had been overshadowed by her husband's stronger personality; now, with him out of town on some errand, not being rushed off as was his habit to do after church, she clearly enjoyed the attention and knowledge that she'd been missed.

What Mary Katherine noticed was that few people asked Miriam about her husband's absence. Maybe it was because they knew the reason....

"So you were talking really seriously with Jenny," her mother said when there was a lull in people stopping by to talk to her.

Mary Katherine found herself thinking about what Jenny had said.

Miriam cleared her throat. "That was a hint."

"Oh, sorry. We just chatted about this and that."

She was grateful when someone interrupted them.... and let her thoughts drift again. Maybe God hadn't talked directly to her. But maybe He'd put Jenny in her path today to talk to her instead. It was something to think about.

Her grandmother had once said that there was a reason why we weren't put on Earth by ourselves. We're supposed to learn something from other people, and they from us, she'd said.

She was in this community for a reason, she was coming to realize, even as it had caused a restlessness in her. This faith-filled community had shaped everything about her—given her stability, loving relationships—well, all but the one with her father. Here she'd grown up with a man who was a friend, then a best friend who understood her better than anyone she knew. A man who wanted a deeper relationship with her but was willing to set aside his own needs so that she could make her own decisions about faith and about spending the rest of her life with him.

She relaxed and breathed in the peaceful atmosphere of after-church here in the house of one of her longtime friends, and when Jacob walked into the room and his eyes searched it for her, she smiled and lifted her hand.

And felt the restlessness leaving her like the tide on a shore.

❖

She was in this community for a reason, she was coming to realize, even as it had caused a restlessness in her. This faith-filled community had shaped everything about her.

Day 1: Taking Every Thought Captive

Read God's Word

For though we live in the world, we do not wage war as the world does. The weapons we fight with are not the weapons of the world. On the contrary, [our weapons] have divine power to demolish strongholds. We demolish arguments and every pretension that sets itself up against the knowledge of God, and we take captive every thought to make it obedient to Christ.

2 Corinthians 10:3-5

Reflect and Respond

What gets you really riled up?

What makes you angry, livid even? What makes you sad? In what instances do you tend to get defensive? When do you tend to be sensitive? What makes you want to break all your dishes or really tell someone what you think of his or her actions?

Christians aren't really supposed to feel any of these strong emotions, right? We're supposed to walk around in a happy stupor, never feeling angry or frustrated or disgusted. That's what a Christian is really supposed to be like, right?

Often we feel like a "less-than" Christian when we're overwhelmed by our emotions. But hear this: emotions are not bad things! God created human beings in His own image, and Scripture talks about God having a range of emotions—happy, sad, angry, compassionate, and so forth.

Emotions are not the enemy. It's natural for us to *feel* things—and we can cycle through many emotions on any given day. But these emotions must not control us or define us; instead, we should examine our emotions as clues about what is going on in our hearts and see them as signposts to show us where God is working in our lives—where He wants us to pay attention.

How do Mary Katherine's emotions—specifically, being restless and frustrated—affect different areas of her life?

We should examine our emotions as clues about what is going on in our hearts and see them as signposts to show us where God is working in our lives.

Do you feel as though you are an emotional person? What are some things that push your buttons and create strong reactions in you?

Reread 2 Corinthians 10:3-5. Think back over the past day or so to a moment when you felt overwhelmed by a particular emotion. What was the emotion?

What was the thought behind the emotion?

In light of this passage, how could you have taken that thought—and consequently, that emotion—captive? What could you have done to step back, consider it, and hand it over to God?

How could you have made that thought—and consequently, that emotion—obedient to Christ? What do you think God wants to reveal to you or teach you through that experience?

When we stop to consider the feelings of restlessness and frustration that often consume us, we generally find that we feel this way because we are looking for satisfaction in things that ultimately can't satisfy us. Our minds may be easily fooled into thinking that we can find fulfillment and satisfaction from the things of this world, but deep down in our hearts we know the truth: the only thing that can fulfill us is the love of God.

In Psalm 63, we find King David hiding out in the desert, on the run from his enemies who are pursuing him with deadly intent. David has known the goodness of God in his success as king, and he has experienced God's provision, presence, love, and favor. Now, in dire straits and facing an uncertain future, it would be tempting for David to feel abandoned by God, to feel frustrated because he is in such a precarious situation. But David knows the only thing that can sustain his hope is the Lord. He says,

> *O God, you are my God,*
> *earnestly I seek you;*
> *my soul thirsts for you,*
> *my body longs for you,*
> *in a dry and weary land*
> *where there is no water.*
> (v. 1)

In the desert of his circumstances, David knows that God will provide for him. Not only does he know that God will provide; he also proclaims that God's provision and love defy every expectation he can imagine.

> *I have seen you in the sanctuary*
> *and beheld your power and your glory.*
> *Because your love is better than life,*
> *my lips will glorify you.*
> *I will praise you as long as I live,*
> *and in your name I will lift up my hands.*
> *My soul will be satisfied as with the richest of foods;*
> *with singing lips my mouth will praise you.*
> (vv. 2-5)

God's love for us, expressed in His work on our behalf through the cross, goes far, far beyond any hope or expectation of love and acceptance we could ever imagine. God pursues our hearts with a relentless love; we are more loved and accepted than we could ever comprehend. He delights in us and is pleased to give us every good thing.

Though Mary Katherine looks to her family and community for approval, those paths simply seem to fuel her frustration and her restlessness. Even her weaving—the craft she loves and finds success in—contributes to her feeling that she doesn't fit well into her farm-centric community. But once she realizes that God loves her, cares for her, and has a plan for her life, she is able to rest in her identity as His child first and foremost. Then she is able to make the big decisions she is facing in life.

God pursues our hearts with a relentless love; we are more loved and accepted than we could ever comprehend.

157

During your time in this study, how have you sensed God saying to you, "Put down your hope in [this thing or person] and find your satisfaction in Me"?

What emotions are driving you these days? How might the Lord be calling to you through these emotions?

Talk to God

Because Your love is better than life, my lips will glorify You, Lord! Help me to put aside my own judgments and expectations so that I may discover that Your love satisfies me more than anything I could ever imagine. Help me to see that You alone are worthy of all my hope and desires, Lord. Show me where I am living under misplaced hope so that I can turn my eyes to You. Thank You for the love and attention You lavish on me. Thank You for pursuing my heart and for redeeming me! Amen.

As You Go

Consider the fruit of the Spirit as described in Galatians 5:22-23. Of the nine characteristics listed here, which are you struggling with today? Ask God to speak to you through this struggle and reveal any thoughts and emotions that need to be turned over to Him.

Day 2: The Author of Reconciliation

Read God's Word

Behold, I will bring to it health and healing, and I will heal them and reveal to them abundance of prosperity and security.

Jeremiah 33:6 ESV

And the peace of God, which surpasses all understanding, will guard your hearts and your minds in Christ Jesus.

Philippians 4:7 ESV

Reflect and Respond

Throughout Scripture, we read beautiful words about God's desire for peace, reconciliation, and healing for His children. As Jesus walked the Earth and ministered to the people around Him, His heart for mercy, healing, and transformation was evident in His every action.

Read the following stories of Jesus' interactions with people who were hurting and in need. What does each story reveal to you about Jesus? How do you see yourself in the story?

John 8:1-11 (Woman caught in adultery)

Matthew 9:18-22 (Woman who touched Jesus' robe)

John 5:1-15 (Man at pool in Bethesda)

Which story do you most strongly identify with and why?

These encounters with Jesus—along with countless others that fill the New Testament—are evidence that God is our great Healer. Just as He heals our bodies, so He longs to heal our hearts and our relationships. With His presence and guidance, broken relationships can be repaired and past hurts can be healed.

In *Her Restless Heart*, we see that as God works in the hearts of Mary Katherine and her parents, Mary Katherine finds she is more and more open to having a restored relationship with her parents. Though she is sifting through years of hurt and pain, Mary Katherine begins to see the hope that God can and will restore their relationship.

Excerpt from Chapter 17

> Just as [God] heals our bodies, so He longs to heal our hearts and our relationships.

Funny thing, Mary Katherine thought. She'd been sitting in church every other Sunday for more than a year now—well, not in a church building but a different home that held church services—and she'd never really heard God speaking to her until she and Jenny had talked that one recent Sunday.

And today.

Well, it wasn't God, exactly. It was Ike, one of the lay ministers, a bookish young man who worked in an RV assembly plant during the day and helped on his family's farm on the weekends.

Looking over the wire-rimmed glasses he wore, he stroked his beard and talked about a passage in Exodus about honoring parents.

Mary Katherine felt some resistance for just a moment, remembering how she and her father had fought that day when he talked of the same thing. Ike spoke of God's love for His children—and His children's love for their children. Generations of love, he said, but sometimes the generations didn't get along because they didn't speak the same language. Their words and their actions weren't what the other used or expected, and so there was distance and misunderstanding. Even anger.

But when we looked beyond these differences in words and actions, he said, used empathy and understanding and forgiveness, we could know a greater love: God's visible love in all areas of our lives.

In Colossians 1:15-22 we read these words:

The Son is the image of the invisible God, the firstborn over all creation. For in him all things were created: things in heaven and on earth, visible and invisible, whether thrones or powers or rulers or authorities; all things have been created through him and for him. He is before all things, and in him all things hold together. And he is the head of the body, the church; he is the beginning and the firstborn from among the dead, so that in every-

thing he might have the supremacy. For God was pleased to have all his fullness dwell in him, and through him to reconcile to himself all things, whether things on earth or things in heaven, by making peace through his blood, shed on the cross.

Once you were alienated from God and were enemies in your minds because of your evil behavior. But now he has reconciled you by Christ's physical body through death to present you holy in his sight, without blemish and free from accusation.

Because God is the author of reconciliation through the perfect sacrifice of Jesus, our desire for peace and unity is fulfilled in Him. Through Jesus' work on the cross, we have been reconciled to God—we have been made pure and whole and right in His sight—and so we are free to extend grace and peace to others.

During this study, has God revealed to you any areas in your life that need reconciliation? If so, how is He leading you to pursue peace in those areas?

With God's help, Mary Katherine is able to begin walking down a path of reconciliation with her parents. How do you think this frees her—to have a life with Jacob, and to pursue the things she loves?

Though God does not guarantee we will have a life free of hurt and pain, what promises does He make in these verses?

Hebrews 13:5

Romans 8:28

Write Hebrews 11:1 below:

In what areas of your life is God asking you to put your faith in Him?

Are you willing to trust Him with the deepest wounds and desires of your heart?

Talk to God

Heavenly Father, You are the great Healer, healing us of our hopeless, sinful state and throwing our sins as far as the east is from the west. Through Your Son's sacrifice, we are healed and made holy and pure in Your sight. Thank You, Lord, for this indescribable gift. Thank You for bringing hope and peace and reconciliation into my life. As You have done for me, bring the same hope into my relationships, Lord, healing past wounds and restoring joy. You are the Author of my life, Lord. Tell Your story of hope through me. Amen.

As You Go

Reflect on Philippians 4:7 today:

And the peace of God, which surpasses all understanding, will guard your hearts and your minds in Christ Jesus. (ESV)

We don't always have to understand how God is working or how He will bring about peace, but we can guard our minds with the knowledge that He *will* do what He promises. How can you claim this truth in your life?

Day 3: Uniquely Gifted

Read God's Word

Whatever you do, work at it with all your heart, as working for the Lord, not for human masters, since you know that you will receive an inheritance from the Lord as a reward.

Colossians 3:23-24a

Whatever you do, do it all for the glory of God.

1 Corinthians 10:31b

Reflect and Respond

When our hearts are able to find peace and satisfaction in God, we are free to be our true selves and live fully in our giftedness. Like Mary Katherine, many of us struggle in life, wondering where we belong. When things don't go perfectly or smoothly, we tend to question ourselves and lose confidence in our abilities.

Though Mary Katherine likes to push the limits of her creativity in her craft by experimenting with new patterns, techniques, and color combinations, she is daunted by the opportunity to speak to a college class about it. Having never set foot on a college campus, she feels unworthy and even a bit embarrassed to think the students will want to hear anything she has to say. But she pushes herself to speak to the class, and it goes great, giving Mary Katherine the confidence she needs to keep working, celebrating her gifts, and finding joy in something that God has gifted her to do.

In Day 3 of Week 3, you listed some of the gifts God has given *you*. How do you utilize and enjoy these gifts?

Over the course of this study, have you sensed God speaking to you about the unique ways in which He has gifted you? In what ways do you feel God is challenging and encouraging you to "push your own limits" and explore those gifts further?

> When our hearts are able to find peace and satisfaction in God, we are free to be our true selves and live fully in our giftedness.

What are some things that might hold you back from exploring and growing in your gifts? How can you give those fears and obstacles to God, asking for His help and guidance?

God delights in the fact that we are all gifted in different ways. He specifically created each of us with different gifts and strengths. If you have children, think about the different gifts and personalities within your family. You would probably acknowledge that, although they may sometimes present challenges and disagreements, the differences that exist between the members make the family stronger, more interesting, and richer. Considering that God has created each of us, it's clear that He feels the same way about us.

Though we can't pick and choose the natural gifts and abilities of our own children, God *can* and *did* choose yours specifically to be used by you. Psalm 139 expresses it so beautifully:

> *You have searched me, L*ORD*, and you know me.*
> *You know when I sit and when I rise; you perceive my thoughts from afar.*
> *You discern my going out and my lying down; you are familiar with all my ways.*
> *...*
> *For you created my inmost being; you knit me together in my mother's womb.*
> *I praise you because I am fearfully and wonderfully made; your works are wonderful, I know that full well.*
> *My frame was not hidden from you when I was made in the secret place, when I was woven together in the depths of the earth.*
> *Your eyes saw my unformed body; all the days ordained for me were written in your book before one of them came to be.*
>
> (vv. 1-3, 13-16)

Read the passage again, this time from *THE MESSAGE* Bible:

> *Oh yes, you shaped me first inside, then out;*
> *you formed me in my mother's womb.*
> *I thank you, High God—you're breathtaking!*
> *Body and soul, I am marvelously made!*

> Though we can't pick and choose the natural gifts and abilities of our own children, God *can* and *did* choose yours specifically to be used by you.

I worship in adoration—what a creation!
You know me inside and out,
  you know every bone in my body;
You know exactly how I was made, bit by bit,
  how I was sculpted from nothing into something.
Like an open book, you watched me grow from conception to birth;
  all the stages of my life were spread out before you,
The days of my life all prepared
  before I'd even lived one day.

(vv. 13-16)

Based on the words of Psalm 139, how do you think God wants us to view the gifts He has given us? Write three descriptions that come to mind.

1.

2.

3.

God wants us to grow in our talents and to be confident of how much He loves us. He wants us to blossom. If we as parents are devoted to fostering and nurturing the talents, abilities, and strengths of our own children, how much more God wants to do that for us! No matter how much we may feel that we don't measure up to some perceived notion of greatness, God regards us as fully approved and accepted. That knowledge should make us rejoice! As such, we are free to try, fail, try again, succeed, and enjoy the process.

God's plan for our gifts is simple:

Whatever you do, work at it with all your heart, as working for the Lord, not for human masters, since you know that you will receive an inheritance from the Lord as a reward.

Colossians 3:23-24a

Whatever you do, do it all for the glory of God.

1 Corinthians 10:31b

165

How is God asking you today to use your gifts for His glory?

Talk to God

God, I praise You that I am fearfully and wonderfully made—YOU made me, equipped me, and blessed me. May I fully understand this wonderful truth, Lord, and embrace it. And may I follow Your lead as You point me toward those things that nurture me and give me life. Amen.

As You Go

As we learn to revel in the gifts we've been given, we also can learn to appreciate and foster the gifts that God has given to others, encouraging and celebrating them rather than being threatened by them. How can you specifically encourage someone else in his or her gifts today?

Day 4: Living Fully in Community

Read God's Word

"For where two or three gather in my name, there am I with them."
Matthew 18:20

Reflect and Respond

We considered the importance of community in Day 5 of Week 3. As our study draws to a close, it is appropriate to revisit the role of community in living fully. There is no denying the wisdom, support, and love that being in community with other believers brings into our lives. Truly living in community—having faith in others and opening ourselves up to them freely and authentically—enriches our lives and challenges us to grow in our faith and blossom as part of the family of God.

For Mary Katherine, her grandmother, Leah, is a steady source of inspiration, strength, and love. Mary Katherine greatly respects Leah's wisdom and perspective, and living with her has helped Mary Katherine to grow. When, after much consideration, Mary Katherine decides to take instruction and join the church, she immediately goes to see Jacob, expecting to share her good news with him. When the encounter is not what she'd hoped for, she hurries home to find Leah.

Excerpt from Chapter 15

The minute [Mary Katherine] got home, she slammed the door, then winced. She should have walked home. Maybe then she'd have gotten rid of some of her pent-up energy. Tears still burned behind her eyelids, and emotions bubbled up inside her.

"Is that you, Mary Katherine?"

Her grandmother came out of the kitchen, wiping her hands on a dish towel. "Oh my goodness, what's the matter?"

Mary Katherine swiped at the tears on her face with her hands. She'd managed not to cry when she hitched a ride with a neighbor, but from the minute she'd climbed out of the buggy, the tears had run unchecked down her cheeks.

Leah dropped the towel and rushed to her side. "Are you hurt? What happened?"

"I went to see the bishop—"

"What did he say? I'll have a word with him!"

"No, no, he didn't hurt me," Mary Katherine said quickly. "It was Jacob!"

"Oh, you quarreled with Jacob." Leah put her arm around her and led her to the kitchen. "Come on, I'll fix you a cup of tea and we'll talk about it."

She shook her head. "You can't cure everything with a cup of tea."

Leah squeezed her shoulders. "No, of course not. It's the talking that goes with it."

She led Mary Katherine to a chair and pushed her gently into it before going to fill the teakettle and set it on the stove.

"Did you have supper?"

Mary Katherine rubbed her forehead and slumped in the chair. "No, first I went to see the bishop, and then I went to see Jacob."

Leah went still and walked over to sit in the chair next to her. "It just sank in. You said you went to see the bishop. What about?"

Chiding herself for not remembering what was most important here, Mary Katherine sat up straighter and reached for her grandmother's hands. "I made plans to take instruction today. I'm joining the church."

Leah closed her eyes, and when she opened them, they were brimming with tears. "Oh, danki, *God! I hoped—oh, how I hoped and prayed," she broke off and dug in the pocket of her dress for a tissue.*

Mary Katherine got to her feet and hugged her. "I never meant to worry you about my decision."

"You didn't. Well, not really." She smiled. "I love what my friend Phoebe says: 'It's arrogant to worry. God knows what He's doing.'"

Her grandmother might deny that she'd worried. But Mary Katherine could feel the trembling in her grandmother's body. It was relief.

When she withdrew her arms, her grandmother stood and bustled around the kitchen, taking out the leftovers from supper and warming them, setting a plate before Mary Katherine and pouring them both a cup of tea.

"Jenny's grandmother," Mary Katherine mused. She propped her elbow on the table and put her chin in her hand. "I guess that's where Jenny gets some of her wisdom. Things she said helped me make my decision."

"Hmm, so is Jenny the only one with a wise grandmother?"

For a moment Mary Katherine was afraid she'd hurt her grandmother's feelings, then she saw the twinkle in her eye.

"No, I, too, have a very wise grandmother."

Unsure if she could eat, Mary Katherine took a bite or two to satisfy her grandmother that she was eating, and then she held the cup of tea in her hands and found comfort in the warmth of the mug.

Her grandmother watched her with kind eyes. "Now tell me, dear one. What has Jacob done to upset you? Wasn't he happy that you'd gone to the bishop?"

Tears welled up again. She set the cup down. "He was upset with me. So upset. Someone had told him that they saw me holding hands with Daniel the other day."

A thought struck her. She remembered being uncomfortable with the way Daniel had taken her hand. She'd hoped no one she knew would see them. And then someone had walked up. Frowning, she tried to remember who it had been. . . .

"This is why I didn't want to get involved with someone." She pressed her hand to her chest. "It wasn't just because I didn't know what I was going to do about joining the church. It just hurts too much to love someone, to place your trust in someone and have them throw it back to you. It hurts too much!"

"So you love Jacob?"

The pain in her chest became sharper as she nodded. She wondered if it was possible to have a heart attack like her mother when she was only in her twenties.

"Give him a little time to cool off," Leah advised. "Sometimes even the best of men don't think before they speak."

The pain and pressure eased as Mary Katherine thought about what her grandmother said, and she found her righteous anger returning. "Oh, I'll give him some time," she muttered darkly. "Because maybe I need to cool off, too!"

Do you have a Leah in your life—someone you go to when you're upset or hurting? Someone who you know will speak wise words to you and help you to gain a different perspective? How has this person affected your life?

Matthew 18:20 says, "For where two or three gather in my name, there am I with them." It is clear that Leah—probably along with her friends—has been praying that Mary Katherine would decide to join the church and stay in the community.

How have you felt the prayers of your community in your life? Can you think of a particular situation when you knew they were praying for you? How did God respond to their prayers, and what did God reveal to you through this situation?

Though she doesn't fit the mold of the "perfect" Amish woman, Mary Katherine decides to stay in her community and marry Jacob. When faced with the choice to stay or to go, Mary Katherine realizes how much love and support she has in her community, and she knows she wants to remain there with them. Having such a solid, loving group of people around her—her grandmother, Leah; cousins Naomi and Anna; Jacob; and even her *Englisch* friend, Jamie—gives Mary Katherine the reassurance that she can be whom God uniquely made her to be, and that her community will support her as she pursues her dreams.

How does Mary Katherine's story encourage you to live fully in *your* community—to both give and receive love and support?

Talk to God

Dear God, thank You that You did not create us to be alone. Though living with others can often be challenging, I thank You for the sweet richness and beauty that others add to my life. Help me to be a friend and a helper to those around me. Show me how to love more deeply, more freely. Thank You for listening to the prayers of Your people, Lord. May we come to You in bold assurance that You hear us when we call. Amen.

As You Go

Are you surrounded by people in your life who you feel support and love you? Do you feel that you are a part of a close community of believers with whom you can share your joys and struggles? If not, ask God to help you find the type of faith community that can help you grow and blossom. If you do have this kind of community, thank God for that gift, and pray that He would show you how you can continue to support and serve others and speak God's love to them.

Day 5: All Things New

Read God's Word

Therefore, if anyone is in Christ, he is a new creation; the old has gone, the new has come!

2 Corinthians 5:17

Do not conform to the pattern of this world, but be transformed by the renewing of your mind. Then you will be able to test and approve what God's will is—his good, pleasing and perfect will.

Romans 12:2

Reflect and Respond

Throughout this study, we have learned about our deep need for love and acceptance, and about how God is able to meet every desire of our hearts. As we see in Mary Katherine's story, when we are able to lay down the fears that hold us hostage and the doubts that so easily hold us back, we will see that God is at work in our lives, actively engaged and laying out a path for us that leads us to walk in closer communion with Him.

When we are secure in the knowledge that we are fully loved and accepted, we can begin to walk that path in freedom, constantly surprised by God's unexpected but wonderful gifts. Second Corinthians 9:8-11 says this:

> *God can pour on the blessings in astonishing ways so that you're ready for anything and everything, more than just ready to do what needs to be done. As one psalmist puts it,*
>
> *He throws caution to the winds,*
> *giving to the needy in reckless abandon.*
> *His right-living, right-giving ways*
> *never run out, never wear out.*
>
> *This most generous God who gives seed to the farmer that becomes bread for your meals is more than extravagant with you. He gives you something you can then give away, which grows into full-formed lives, robust in God, wealthy in every way, so that you can be generous in every way, producing with us great praise to God.*
>
> *(THE MESSAGE)*

As God begins to open Mary Katherine's heart and calm her fears, she discovers wonderful surprises that God has in store for her—the love of a wonderful man and fulfilling work.

Have you ever been surprised by God? How? What happened?

When we are able to lay down the fears that hold us hostage and the doubts that so easily hold us back, we will see that God is at work in our lives, actively engaged and laying out a path for us....

In what way is God leading you to be bold and courageous, trusting that He has everything under control and is working it for good?

How is God calling you to respond?

Reread 2 Corinthians 9:11. What is God extravagantly giving you so that you can give it away to others?

Our Father, the
Great Restorer,
makes all things
new in His time.

Mary Katherine's journey isn't easy or predictable, but her struggles prove necessary and worthy because they lead her closer to the heart of God. There she can rest and be renewed by His love and affection, free of binding fear and nagging doubt.

Our Father, the Great Restorer, makes all things new in His time. We need only listen and respond. Hear these words from Romans 12:1-2:

> *. . . Take your everyday, ordinary life—your sleeping, eating, going-to-work, and walking-around life—and place it before God as an offering. Embracing what God does for you is the best thing you can do for him. Don't become so well-adjusted to your culture that you fit into it without even thinking. Instead, fix your attention on God. You'll be changed from the inside out. Readily recognize what he wants from you, and quickly respond to it. Unlike the culture around you, always dragging you down to its level of immaturity, God brings the best out of you, develops well-formed maturity in you.*
>
> *(THE MESSAGE)*

What relationships or situations in *Her Restless Heart* illustrate God's ability to renew and restore?

How do you personally identify with these stories?

How is God asking you to live fully today, free of fear and hesitation?

How is He prompting you to try new things and step out on a limb, trusting Him to see you through?

What have you learned through this study about trusting in God and resting in His love for you?

Talk to God

I praise You, Lord. Thank You for Your goodness and faithfulness to me. I rejoice that I can trust You fully, Lord, with all my heart and soul—with my very life. Renew me, Lord. Give me boldness, strength, and confidence—evidence of a life lived by trusting in You. Help me to run to You when the doubts and fears of life are too much, Lord, so that I may receive Your peace and assurance and live fully and freely in You. Amen.

As You Go

Revelation 21:5 proclaims, "He who was seated on the throne said, 'I am making everything new!' Then he said, 'Write this down, for these words are trustworthy and true.'" Take some time today to write down the words that God has been speaking to you through your time in this study of His Word.

About the Amish

How is conflict handled in the Amish community?

The bishop of a church is often consulted in matters of conflict, but there is usually little conflict in an Amish community. When you attend church every other week in the home of a church member and often work together to help one another in the community, you realize that petty things do not matter. The good of the church and community is more important. Family is vitally important in the community; often families are interrelated, with cousins several times removed marrying and starting families of their own.

Why are intergenerational relationships so important in the Amish community?

Amish children learn from a young age to respect the elder members of their family and look to them for wisdom. For the most part, families stay in the community, so children have a chance to be cherished by their grandparents and great-grandparents. Everyone shares in the activities that help the community, such as barn raisings and harvests and so on. Faith is uppermost. Family members are cherished and traditions are followed. Relationships are built on these strong foundations.

Video Notes
A Few Minutes with Barbara

Interesting Insights:

Points I'd Like to Discuss with the Group:

Notes

Week 1

1. Matthew Henry, "Psalm 46," in *Matthew Henry Commentary on the Whole Bible* (1706; BibleStudyTools.com, 2012), http://www.biblestudytools.com/commentaries/matthew-henry-complete/psalms/46.html

2. St. Augustine, *The Confessions of St. Augustine, Bishop of Hippo* (398; Cyber Library, 2002), bk. I, chap. I, http://www.leaderu.com/cyber/books/augconfessions/bk1.html

3. "Amish Studies," The Young Center for Anabaptist and Pietist Studies at Elizabethtown College, accessed October 18, 2012, http://www2.etown.edu/amishstudies/

4. "How Do the Amish Help Haiti?," Amish America, posted January 23, 2010, http://amishamerica.com/how-do-the-amish-help-haiti/

Week 2

1. William Faulkner, *Requiem for a Nun* (1951), Act I, scene iii.

2. Oscar Wilde. "A Woman of No Importance," Act II, in Beckson and Fong, eds., *The Complete Works of Oscar Wilde*, vol. 7 (New York: Oxford UP), 249.

Week 3

1. Macrina Wiederkehr, quoted in M. S. Ryan, ed., *A Grateful Heart* (New York: Fine Communications), 71.

Recipes from
the Stitches in Time Series

Jacob's Macaroni and Cheese

Preheat oven to 350 degrees.

1/4 cup butter or margarine (reserve 1 tablespoon)
1/4 cup flour
1 cup milk
8 ounces (1/2 pound) Velveeta cut in small cubes
2 cups cooked elbow macaroni (or any shape macaroni)
1/2 cup shredded cheddar cheese (sharp or mild)
Optional: 6 buttery crackers (Ritz), crushed

Melt 3 tablespoons butter in a pan on low heat. Add flour. Stir and cook for about two minutes. Add milk and stir. Bring to a boil without burning. Gradually add the Velveeta; stir until melted. Add macaroni. Pour into baking dish that has been sprayed with cooking spray or greased with some butter or margarine. Sprinkle with the cheddar. Mix remaining tablespoon butter or margarine with crumbled crackers; then sprinkle over the casserole.

Set timer for 20 minutes (this is very important). Bake casserole until heated through and top cracker crust is browned.

Amish Coffee Cake

1/4 pound butter, softened
1 cup sugar
2 large eggs
2 cups flour
1/4 teaspoon salt
1 teaspoon baking powder
1 teaspoon baking soda
1 cup sour cream
1 teaspoon vanilla or almond extract

Topping
1/2 cup light brown sugar
1 teaspoon cinnamon

Cream the butter, sugar, and eggs. Add flour, salt, baking powder, and soda together; then add sour cream and vanilla. Pour entire mixture into baking pan. Mix topping ingredients and sprinkle over the butter. Bake for 30 minutes or until done.

Amish Zucchini Bread

3 cups flour
1 cup sugar
4 1/2 teaspoons baking powder
1 teaspoon salt
4 ounces chopped nuts (walnuts or pecans)
4 ounces raisins
3 eggs
2/3 cup oil
2 cups shredded zucchini

Mix ingredients (don't over-mix) and pour into two loaf pans. Bake for 1 hour or until done. Cool for at least 15 minutes before taking out of pans, and then cool completely on wire racks.

Three Bear Soup
(Great for sick kids!)

3 tablespoons olive oil
1 onion, diced
1 pound stew meat or lean hamburger
2 large carrots, diced
3 stalks celery, diced
1 16-ounce package frozen mixed vegetables
1 28-ounce can whole peeled tomatoes, juice included
1 teaspoon salt
1/2 teaspoon pepper
1 teaspoon dried parsley
2 quarts beef or vegetable broth

Saute onion, meat, carrots, and celery until meat is no longer pink. Add remaining ingredients and bring to a boil; then reduce heat and simmer for at least an hour (two hours is even better). Serve at a temperature that is not too hot or too cool but just right, and watch sick kids perk up.

Soup is even better the next day.

Alphabet macaroni or seashell macaroni may be added.

White Hot Chocolate

1 cup white chocolate chips
1 cup heavy cream
4 cups half-and-half
1 teaspoon vanilla extract
Peppermint sticks or candy canes (optional)

Place chips in a saucepan over medium heat. Add cream and stir until chips are melted. Add half-and-half and extract. Serve warm with peppermint sticks or candy canes as stirrers.

FLORIDA RECIPES

Shrimp and Grits

1 cup stone-ground grits
2 cups water
2 cups milk
1 teaspoon Old Bay seasoning
2 cloves garlic, finely minced
6 tablespoons butter
4 slices bacon, finely diced
4 cloves garlic, finely diced or minced
1 large onion, chopped
1 tablespoon all-purpose flour
1 pound pink Gulf shrimp
3/4 cup water, divided
1/2 teaspoon Old Bay seasoning
2 tablespoons seafood or vegetable bouillon granules

Heat 2 cups water, milk, 1 teaspoon Old Bay, garlic, and 3 tablespoons butter to almost boiling in a medium saucepan. Add grits and cook for 6-8 minutes, stirring occasionally. Meanwhile, in a separate skillet, melt the other three tablespoons of butter and saute bacon, garlic, and onion. When lightly browned, add flour and make a basic roux. Stir until fully blended. Add shrimp and 1/4 cup water, 1/2 teaspoon Old Bay, and bouillon. Simmer until gravy thickens. Serve grits with shrimp and gravy. This makes a delicious dish for brunch or supper.

Recipe by Sherry Gore, Pinecraft, Florida
—From *Taste of Pinecraft: Glimpses of Sarasota, Florida's Amish Culture and Kitchens* by Sherry Gore

Fruity Florida Coleslaw

2 Florida oranges (or canned mandarin oranges)
2 apples, chopped
1 head shredded cabbage
1 cup red grapes
1/4 cup coconut flakes
1/2 cup chopped walnuts
1 whole banana, sliced
1 (16 oz.) can pineapple chunks, drained
dash of salt
1/2 cup mayonnaise
3/4 cup whipped topping
1 tablespoon sugar
1 tablespoon lemon juice

Place cabbage, fruits, and nuts in large bowl. In small bowl, mix remaining ingredients well. Pour over cabbage mixture and serve in your prettiest glass dish.

Recipe by Shannon Gore, Pinecraft, Florida
—From *Taste of Pinecraft: Glimpses of Sarasota, Florida's Amish Culture and Kitchens* by Sherry Gore

Key Lime Pie

1 8-inch baked pie crust
1/2 cup fresh lime juice
1 14-ounce can sweetened condensed milk
1 1/2 to 2 cups Cool Whip
Green food coloring (optional)
Additional Cool Whip

Beat lime juice and condensed milk together. Add Cool Whip and food coloring and pour into pie crust. Top with additional Cool Whip. Fresh lemon juice will work same as lime.

Recipe by Laura Yoder, Sarasota, Florida
—From *Taste of Pinecraft: Glimpses of Sarasota, Florida's Amish Culture and Kitchens* by Sherry Gore

Another Great Bible Study from the Faith and Fiction Series

Popular Christian fiction author Melody Carlson draws upon her novels in the Inn at Shining Waters trilogy to invite women on an exciting journey toward healing. Using the stories, themes, and characters of the novels as a backdrop—much in the way that Jesus used stories to teach important truths and principles—this 8-week, DVD-based study explores the need for forgiveness and mercy in our lives and the role that second chances and new beginnings play in healing our spirits and our relationships. *Abingdon Press.*

Participant Book • Leader Guide • DVD

Melody Carlson is the award-winning author of more than two hundred books and the recipient of a Romantic Times Career Achievement Award and a Rita Award. She and her husband live in Central Oregon.

For more information, visit AbingdonPress.com, AbingdonWomen.com, or your favorite Christian retailer.

God Wants to Rewrite Your Story

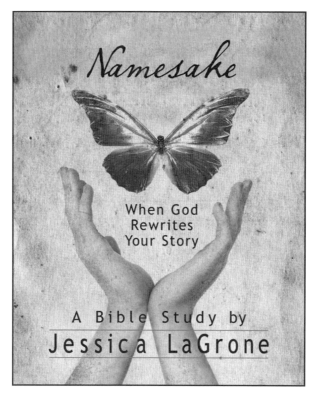

Meet popular author, speaker, blogger, and pastor Jessica LaGrone—a dynamic new voice in in-depth Bible study. In her six-week Bible study, Namesake, she explores the power of God to transform our lives and destinies by focusing on six biblical stories about persons who encountered God and whose names and lives were forever changed. As you meet Abraham, Sarah, Jacob, Naomi, Daniel, Peter, and an un-named woman, you will discover that God wants to be just as intimately involved in your own story, offering an identity that shines with the purpose for which you were created—to know Him through His Son, Jesus, and to become more and more like Him, bringing God glory for His name's sake.

Participant Book • Leader Guide • DVD • Mini Preview Book
Leader Kit (includes one of each component)

Jessica LaGrone is Pastor of Worship at The Woodlands United Methodist Church in The Woodlands, Texas. An acclaimed preacher, teacher, and writer— including her popular blog "Reverend Mother" (jessicalagrone.com)—she enjoys speaking at retreats and events at churches throughout the United States. She and her husband, Jim, have two young children, Drew and Kate.

For more information, visit AbingdonPress.com, AbingdonWomen.com, or your favorite Christian retailer.

Be Transformed by God's Love and Acceptance

Every woman longs to know that she is loved, accepted, and valued. Yet, many wonder, "Does God really love me as I am? Do I really matter to God?" In this 8-week Bible study, award-winning gospel singer, songwriter, and teacher Babbie Mason helps women of all ages and walks of life to discover the depth and breadth of God's great love and acceptance. Drawing upon her own personal journey to understand how much God loves her—not as a singer or teacher but as God's beloved daughter—she equips women to accept God's unfailing love as they understand and claim seven biblical promises.

Participant Book • Leader Guide • DVD • Mini Preview Book
Leader Kit (includes one of each component plus a bonus music CD)

Babbie Mason is a Dove Award-winning, Grammy-nominated, American Gospel singer and songwriter; a tireless women's conference speaker; a worship leader through her Embrace: A Worship Celebration for Women concerts; adjunct professor of songwriting at Lee University; television talk-show host of *Babbie's House*; and a published author. The parents of two adult sons, Babbie and her husband, Charles, live on a farm in West Georgia.

Barbara Cameron is the author of more than 30 fiction and nonfiction books, three nationally televised movies (HBO-Cinemax), and is the winner of the first Romance Writers of America Golden Heart Award. When a relative took her to visit the Amish community in Lancaster, Pennsylvania, she felt led to write about the spiritual values and simple joys she witnessed there. She currently resides in Edgewater, Florida.

Follow Barbara on  *Facebook,*
or find out more about her and her work at
www.BarbaraCameron.com, www.AmishHearts.com,
and www.AmishLiving.com.